ALONE
with
GOD

Other Spiritual Publications by John Andrew Gallery

SELF-PUBLISHED

Living in the Kingdom of God
Second Edition, 2021
(Eleven core teachings from the
parables and sayings of Jesus of Nazareth)

On Love
(Pamphlet, 2018)

On Generosity
(Pamphlet, 2019)

PENDLE HILL PAMPHLETS

Be Patterns
Reflections on words of George Fox
Pamphlet 473, 2022

Wait and Watch
Spiritual Practice, Rehearsal, and Performance
Pamphlet 485, 2024

www.johnandrewgallery.com

ALONE with *GOD*

SPIRITUAL REFLECTIONS
AND ESSAYS
2000–2024

John Andrew Gallery

Philadelphia 2025

ALONE WITH GOD
Spiritual Reflections and Essays, 2000–2024
© 2025 John Andrew Gallery

ISBN (paperback): 978-1-7367180-3-2
ISBN (e-book): 978-1-7367180-4-9

All rights reserved.
No part of this publication may be reproduced in any form
by any electronic or mechanical means without permission in
writing from the author, except in the case of brief quotations
in book reviews, magazine articles, or similar publications and
certain non-commercial uses permitted by copyright law. For
permission contact John via *www.johnandrewgallery.com/contact*.

All quotations from the gospels are from the King James Version
of the New Testament.

Reflections from Pendle Hill Pamphlets 358 and 469,
and quotations from Pamphlet 264, included with permission
of Pendle Hill Publications.

Grateful appreciation to Duane Michals for permission to use
image #3 from his sequence *The Spirit Leaves the Body* (1968).

Contents

Introduction	*1*
Sowing Peace	*5*
Clouds	*10*
A Fool for God	*14*
Rain	*18*
This is My Prayer	*22*
The Peace of God	*27*
April Fools	*31*
On Timothy McVeigh	*34*
Praying for One Another	*39*
Grounded	*42*
Being Faithful	*46*
Shepherds in the Fields	*50*
A Thief in the Night	*55*
A Song of Peace	*57*
Thinking Ahead	*60*
There is Another Way	*64*
Independence Day Blues	*68*
Farewell Flyby	*70*

At the Movies: Reflections on the Testimony of Honesty/Integrity	*71*
On Love	*82*
Holy Saturday Meditation	*90*
At the Movies 2: Reflections on Leadings and Spiritual Journeys	*95*
Sisyphus	*104*
Holding in the Light	*108*
Entering the Stream	*111*
Easter Sunday	*114*
Time and the River	*118*
Sitting with Jesus	*121*
Finding the Way to Walk	*124*
Cherry Blossoms	*127*
Trust and Serve	*131*
Alone with God	*134*
There is a Crack in Everything	*139*
Tree Energy	*143*
Christ in the Midst	*146*
Siddhartha	*149*
Black Jesus	*153*
Marcus Aurelius	*159*
Eid al-Adha	*163*
Healing Begins	*168*
Look for the Good	*172*

Hope	*174*
The Certainty of Faith	*177*
Holding in the Light 2	*181*
Leaping into the Void	*184*
Two Meditations: On the Intrusion of the Divine into My Daily Life	*186*
Sitting with Jesus 2	*189*
Accidents	*198*
Welcoming Temptation	*203*
Enjoy Your Life	*210*
The Life of the Spirit	*215*
To Err is Human; To Forgive is Human Too	*223*
Two Practical Commandments	*233*
Fatherly Love	*237*
The Courage of a Caterpillar	*245*
Such Thought Have I	*250*
Acknowledgments	*261*
Citations	*263*
About the Author	*269*

Introduction

WRITING SPIRITUAL REFLECTIONS is not something I ever expected to do. It was something I was led to do in a very casual way, but once I began it became, and has continued to be, an important part of my spiritual practice.

I call the majority of what I have written "reflections" because that is how they came about: they are the written record of the thoughts and associations that came to mind as I reflected on a specific event that occurred during the day on which the reflection was written.

The 56 reflections included in this collection were inspired by three different experiences. The initial impetus came from my participation in a prayer vigil for peace that I and several other Quakers held on Independence Mall in Philadelphia beginning in 1999. When the NATO bombing of Kosovo began, I felt a strong need to do something visible to express my concern. Other Friends felt similarly and the idea of a prayer vigil on Sunday afternoons quickly emerged. Over the five years I participated in the vigil it became an important part of my spiritual practice. Simply standing in a public place, with a sign that read "Pray for Peace," deepened my understanding of what it takes to be a peaceful person in the face of a seemingly indifferent—and often hostile—world.

Two of the other participants conceived of the idea of writing weekly reports to email to others who wanted to support us but could not attend in person. They invited me to contribute and so on Sunday evenings before going to bed I started writing short email reflections about some aspect of my experience that day.

There was something about writing late at night that was particularly inspiring. The world around me was asleep; there were no voices of people passing by, no sounds of cars or buses rushing through the streets outside. The darkness of night seemed to spread a blanket of silence and stillness over everything that enveloped me as well. I sat in a small pool of light, an island in that darkness, seemingly alone but not alone. There was another presence that was the source of the words that came to me in a way they didn't come in the light of day. The words seemed to flow through my arm to the pen, and then across the page, as if I were merely an instrument, inspired by a source beyond my conscious control.

Although each reflection began with a specific event from my day, the spiritual implications of that event brought forth ideas from many spiritual teachers whose words I had read, and from some sources that would not normally be considered spiritual at all—as you will discover as you read along.

Twenty years later, under very different circumstances, I had a similar experience. When the 2020 Covid-19 pandemic forced me into self-isolation in the privacy of my apartment, I began holding what I called a solitary meeting for worship on Sunday morning at the same time I would have been attending Quaker meeting. In the absence of the type of external influences I experienced during the vigil, I expected that it would simply be a time of silent meditation. But I forgot one thing: once again, I was not alone. God was present again and prepared to use other instruments to bring me words I needed to hear and to share. The objects around me—books, statues, birds, music—seemed to send off a vibration that resonated within me and brought forth a complimentary vibration that gave rise to an unexpected spiritual thought. At the end of the day, I found myself once again writing reflections and once again drawing on ideas from a wide range of spiritual and non-spiritual sources.

In between those two events, and continuing after 2020, the random experiences of my daily life led to other reflections, as well as longer essays on specific topics that often came to me from unexpected sources.

Since these reflections and essays were written over an extended period of time, without reference to one another, there is a certain amount of repetition of themes, language, and quotations. I have chosen to leave them as they were originally written, for they represent the spiritual path along which I have been led over the past twenty-four years. They can be read straight through, from beginning to end, as a book is usually read. However, because they are short and written to stand alone, independent of one another, they can be read individually (as they were originally) and in any order—one a day or two or three a week as a source of inspiration for personal reflection on the themes and ideas each contains.

Reading them over again has made me realize that the issues and themes I wrote about are still relevant to my spiritual journey; I hope they will be relevant to, and a source of inspiration for yours as well.

Sowing Peace

January 2000
Friends Journal and Pendle Hill Pamphlet 358

ON SUNDAY, AS we maintained our weekly peace vigil on Independence Mall, I reflected on a lesson I had prepared to teach in First-day school that morning. The First-day school is studying the parables of Jesus, and I had reflected on the parable of the sower some of whose seeds are eaten by birds, some fall on rock or in weeds, while others fall on fertile ground. This parable is usually interpreted in terms of the seeds as a symbol for the Word of God. After all, this is how the Gospel says Jesus himself explained it. That might be true, and there are useful ideas that can be learned from looking at the parable that way. But for me this parable, like others, illustrates the characteristics of a man (and most of them are about men) who is already living in the Kingdom of God, even as he goes about his daily life. The parable is a means of showing how we too should live if we want to live in the Kingdom of God.

This parable is very simple. The man goes out to the field, he throws his grain, some is eaten by birds, some falls on rock, some may grow up among weeds, and some will fall on fertile ground and bring forth a good harvest. To Jesus's listeners this must have seemed a strange story—after all, it is exactly what any one of them would have done in planting a field, a perfectly ordinary act and way of sowing in those times. How does this seemingly ordinary story tell us anything about living in the Kingdom of God?

I find it useful to look at the parables in contrast to the way I might do something similar. I have often planted a vegetable garden. When I do, I first create some rows in the soil and then carefully sprinkle my seeds down each row, trying to make sure there is adequate space between each seed. I cover them over and water them. I am trying to make sure that each and every seed I plant grows. Of course, I know that this will not be the case, and that even if they all did grow, they would be too close together, and I would have to weed out some. But my planting actions are based on a desire on my part to control the results of my actions—to ensure that every seed grows.

The sower in the parable takes a very different approach. He *knows* that every seed may not grow—some will fall on rocks, some will have to be weeded out, some may not get enough water or sun. He knows that if he tried to control what happens to each seed it would be pointless, and what's more, it would take him forever to plant his fields. So, he acts quite differently than I do in two important ways. First, he doesn't try to control the outcome of his actions; he isn't overly concerned with the results. He knows that if he throws enough seeds in generally the right direction, enough will fall on fertile ground to create a good harvest. Second, he trusts God. He trusts God that enough will fall on fertile ground, and that the rain and sun will come. Those two things—not being overly concerned with results and trusting God—are the difference between him and me, the difference between someone who is living in the Kingdom of God and someone who is still trying to.

Not being concerned with results is hard for me. Sometimes I am hesitant to do something unless I am fairly certain I will succeed. In many cases, not being certain, I don't try. When I do try, I often want the results to be what I want. I'm not always prepared to trust the process, to trust God, that a result different from what I think is best is, in fact, best.

This parable helped me understand more clearly what I am doing by participating in the peace vigil. I started last April because I felt a need to take an action that expressed my concern about the NATO bombings. What was the right action? I use that term in its Buddhist sense. The right action was to be a visible reminder that peace is the essential goal. The sower takes right action: To feed his family and village he must plant his field, and to be successful he must throw his seed at least in the right direction. So, the first action is *deciding* on right action. For Quakers this is sometimes characterized as a leading, but that sounds overly serious to me.

The second action is *taking* action. It's not enough to know what's right to do; you actually have to do it. The sower sows his grain; I and others stand in the cold holding signs. What results do I expect from my actions? Do I expect NATO to stop bombing in the Balkans because of what I am doing? No. Do I expect President Clinton and Congress to change their views? No. I have no idea what the results may be; I don't care. I am simply trusting God that some good may come of this.

Each week some collection of people reacts to us. Some stop and talk; some honk horns and give us a thumbs-up. This past Sunday a group of Asian tourists stopped and looked at us, talking in their own language to one another. With motions, they asked if they could take our picture. We have become used to that. But these people wanted to be *in* the photo. One woman came forward and stood beside me and had her picture taken; a man came and stood next to Marcelle and had his; two people picked up signs and stood in front of us and had their picture taken. As they were doing this, I thought about what would happen when they got home, thousands of miles away. They would take out their pictures and show them to their friends and in the midst of all their views of the United States they would come across these—"Oh, look," they would say; "Remember those Quakers in Philadelphia standing in the cold for peace?" (We gave them some Quaker literature.) What will their friends think? Who's to know that the pictures won't encourage one or more of them to make a more serious commitment to peace in their own lives?

By standing on the mall, I throw my seeds. I am not

concerned with the results. I trust that God will find some fertile ground for them to fall on, and each seed that grows—each person who goes away reminded that peace is our goal—will eventually produce an incredible harvest.

Clouds

March 2000
Pendle Hill Pamphlet 358

IN THE LATE AFTERNOON the tall buildings west of Independence Mall cast long shadows over the place where we stand in front of the Liberty Bell pavilion. We look north, directly into the shadows, and then beyond into the sky illuminated by the strong late-afternoon light. On this day, my eyes and mind drift back and forth between the people on the street and the sky above them. The street scene, the buildings, and the people are all a dark gray tone; the sky above is mostly blue, the color paint stores might call "sky blue."

For the most part, the sights and sounds are the same as on other days: cars speed by and you can hear some people laughing loudly through open windows and I wonder if that is directed toward us; teenage boys glide by on skateboards, look at us, and smile, and I wonder what they are thinking. Each week there is at least one person who catches my attention. This week it is an Asian American teenage boy. He rides by on his mountain bike, earphones on his head, listening to some music we cannot hear. His trip from my right to left and out of my field of vision takes just one minute. But in that minute he glances at us, reads the signs, nods his head, and holds one hand high, fist clenched in agreement and support of our cause. And then he's gone.

Except for him, it was the sky that held my attention. Against the incredible blue sky, I watched white clouds drift by. They looked exactly like big balls of cotton—so real that I felt I could reach up and touch them. Yet I knew that if I tried, I would only grasp moist air. The clouds drift from left to right in my view, ever so slowly, as if they had infinite patience. By the time they have reached the other side of my field of vision often they have changed. Some merely change shape, but some fall apart and there will be several clouds drifting on where once there was one. Sometimes they fall apart completely and disappear entirely in the few minutes that it takes them to travel the equivalent of crossing from 6th to 5th street. They have come from China and look down with equal serenity on everything they pass over; they will drift on to Europe, then Russia, with the same indifference.

Lately I've become quite preoccupied with clouds. I stop as I walk through the city streets and look up and see these gleaming white shapes—huge, puffed up, incredible, magical shapes—sometimes drifting by at their ease, sometimes racing by, driven by a wind I cannot feel. Often in these moments I stop and say to myself, Dear God, how did you ever think of something as wonderful as clouds? But I know God didn't; what I call God merely put some things in place—in this case sun and air and water—and provided an opportunity for something to happen, something unexpected or unplanned. God would have been equally pleased as I at the beauty of the clouds and just as surprised the first time they appeared—well, not surprised perhaps, because the potential for such a phenomenon existed in what had been created from the start.

This is how I think of my life. God has put things out there for me to interact with, and when I am in harmony with God these interactions produce wonderful and unexpected results. Standing on the mall is part of that: placing myself there and waiting for whatever it is I'm supposed to interact with to show up, this day that being clouds. Looking up at the clouds gives me a sense of scale and of the larger universe that looking at the street scene and the physical environment around me obscures. To be outside in the natural world brings me back to a sense of myself as a creature, just a small creature and one of many, in this world, this universe, vibrating in harmony with all the others. In these moments I can easily say with Jesus, "I and my father are one."

Being in the natural world inspires my spiritual thought. In Buddhism there is the concept of entering the stream. The development of a spiritual life has many stages. One is the equivalent of sitting by the stream and admiring it, much as I admire the clouds. We want a spiritual life and even just to want it is inspiring, but that's all we do, sit and watch. The next stage is like putting your toes in the water, just testing it. To me that's equivalent to praying or meditating occasionally or showing up for meeting for worship when it's convenient. But that isn't enough to move forward. Entering the stream, for a Buddhist, means making a serious commitment to a spiritual life by making a commitment to consistent spiritual practice. You haven't yet achieved a spiritual life or even given yourself over to it fully, but entering the stream, feeling the cold water on your legs, and taking those steps is the start. It's like setting your hand to the plow and not looking back. There is one more stage which, for me, is lying down in the water, floating, letting the current of the stream carry you as it would carry a leaf. This is the surrender to God that makes all else possible: complete peace, complete surrender to the current of the universe and where it carries you.

Where am I? Sometimes it seems I'm just standing on the riverbank watching the stream, just as I'm standing on the street corner watching the clouds. Sometimes it seems I'm just getting my toes wet by standing on the mall with a sign.

I imagine Jesus in the same situation—sitting on the bank of the Jordan River watching John baptize. I wonder what it was in that moment, in that time of his life, in that place, on that particular day, with that particular man, with the blue sky above filled with white clouds—what it was that led him to enter the stream.

A Fool for God

June 2000
Friends Journal and Pendle Hill Pamphlet 358

EACH SUNDAY I've gone to the vigil I've wondered what would happen if no one else showed up. Would I be willing to stand there alone with my sign? Would I have the patience to stay the whole hour, alone, or would I tire more easily and leave early since no one would really know? How would I handle, alone, the people who might stop and talk? How would I handle the indifferent stares of those who just pass by me?

This Sunday I had a small taste of that. For 10 to 15 minutes I stood alone. I knew that Dan was there, finding quarters for the parking meter, and that I would not have to stand the full hour by myself. But in those 10 to 15 minutes I experienced at least some minor part of what I had often wondered about.

Throughout my life I've seen individuals on the street carrying signs with religious messages. My first thought used to be (and I confess, often still is) "religious crackpot." There are some of whom I think differently—Jehovah's Witnesses handing out their magazine or individuals giving out small pamphlets printed by the Street Bible Tract Association. I admire their courage and ability to witness to their beliefs so publicly.

Generally, I say of myself, I couldn't do that. But others strike me differently. In Philadelphia I often see people around City Hall carrying signs. The messages invariably go back to John the Baptist (Repent, the end is near!). Some invoke Jesus's name (Only Jesus Saves from Sin, on a carefully lettered sign nailed to a tree that I see each morning on my trip to work) or make reference to a passage of scripture—usually something from the Gospel of John like the signs you occasionally see at baseball games when the TV camera scans the crowd (John 5:10–14, or something similar). I look at these people and think they've lost a part of their sanity. What fools they are, I say to myself, to believe that such actions have any value, any impact. And that's what I imagine people would think of me if I were standing alone with my sign "Pray for Peace in the World" with a list below of the word for peace in all the languages I could find in the foreign language dictionary section of my local bookstore.

Am I prepared to be a fool for God? In the Tarot deck, the Fool is the first of the major arcana—number zero, no-thing. He is depicted as a carefree young man in a richly colorful dress carrying a rose in one hand and a stick in the other from which is suspended an embroidered purse. He stands on a high mountain ledge under bright sunshine gazing happily into the distance with his little dog jumping beside him. "He is the prince of the other world on his travels through this one," one explanation reads; "He is spirit in search of experience." For me he is, in many respects, the personification of

George Fox's phrase "walk cheerfully over the world, answering that of God in everyone." The explanations of the card say that the Fool calls to the child inside of us, the part of us that wants to act intuitively, instinctively, even impulsively, spontaneously, joyously, without fear. To me, he seems to be child in spirit, living completely in the present moment, in total unity with God and in joyous harmony with all creation. He seems to fully represent such thoughts as "Unless you are like a little child you shall not enter the Kingdom of God" (He's entered!), and "If the birds don't worry about where their next day's food will come from why should you?" (He doesn't worry!) One can easily say that anyone who truly tries to live by Jesus's teachings—anyone who tries to live in the Kingdom—will be viewed as a fool in the eyes of the world. So, yes, then, I must be willing to be like him, a fool for God.

As I stood alone, only I felt different. Those who ignored me and rushed past to see the Liberty Bell or were heading home from the bike race, would have ignored all of us. Those who looked and paused would have looked and paused at all of us. One African American woman walked slowly by. She read the signs I had propped up against the building, then read mine. She looked a lot like Whoopi Goldberg. Around her neck she wore a plain, dark wooden cross suspended on a leather string. She looked at me and softly said "Bless you" as she walked on. No, she did not think me a fool, just a fool for God.

I often struggle with my feelings about the people

who pass. It's easy to become judgmental: there are "them" (the ones who ignore us and go about their business) and "us" (those who pause, read, talk, make a positive sign of acknowledgement or take a picture). It's easy to forget that we are called to love them all. At the end of the hour, Tony brought me back to this when he shared his reflection. He said he often found himself classifying the people who passed: this one understands that one doesn't, etc. He didn't like that judgmental feeling any more than I do. So, he decided that he would look directly at each person and pray for that person for as long as the person looked at us. Thus, everyone became the object of his love and prayer—even those who just glanced and walked past. Those who walked more slowly, looked and read, got the benefit of a longer prayer. It was a powerful reminder that we are called to love them all—all whom we meet each day of our lives—and to pray for their well-being. May you be happy, Buddha used to say as a blessing to someone leaving.

We are called to love them all—supporters, opponents, interested, disinterested, wealthy, poor, all. And if that makes us fools for God, so be it.

Rain

August 2000
Pendle Hill Pamphlet 358

At 4PM as I arrive the sky is pale gray; it could rain, but it just as easily could not. I take an umbrella from the car just in case. As soon as I take my place in line with the others, I hear thunder in the distance, to the southwest. It's infrequent and almost sounds like the noise of fireworks that go off early in the show when they are let off slowly and individually. Over the course of 30 minutes the sounds become more frequent, grow louder, and are clearly moving toward us. Yet the sky doesn't change; it remains pale gray. I stand there knowing a storm is approaching and that if it comes I and the others will continue to stand peacefully with our signs. I am remarkably at peace with that, with the prospect that maybe I'll get wet.

At 4:30 a few drops fall, and all the tourists run for cover. In a matter of minutes it's pouring heavily, and it continues like that for 20 minutes. Straight ahead, over North Philadelphia, I can see bolts of lightning coming down to earth almost parallel to the lightning bolt in Noguchi's sculpture at the foot of the Ben Franklin Bridge. The rain is beautiful and intense. My small umbrella doesn't keep it all out and water splashes all around me. My legs, sandals, feet get soaked while others, standing calmly without protection, get soaked completely. As I am watching this I am reminded of a Buddhist thought about anger: "I am the landscape, not the storm." We are like that. We stand as calmly as the trees, bend with the wind, accept the rain, and in 20 minutes it's over—the sky is blue, there are big white fluffy clouds, and the sun is shining.

About a half hour later, after the vigil is over but while we were meeting, a few drops fell again, and the sky quickly darkened as if the earlier storm was just an appetizer and here comes the main course. The thunder was intense, cracking directly overhead almost as if we could expect a lightning bolt to land right there at our feet. There is something wonderful about the image of an angry God hurling lightning bolts from the sky; it makes me treasure the Greek myths and Zeus, with his quiver of lightning bolts ready at hand. The rain that followed was intense, it flooded the streets, quickly forming little rivers along the edge of the curb. And then, 20 minutes later it's over. The storm is gone; the landscape remains.

In the novel *Dune*, the lead character, Paul, says this prayer in times of fear: "Fear is the mind-killer. Fear is the little-death that brings total obliteration. I will face my fear. I will permit it to pass over me and through me. And when it has gone past I will turn the inner eye to see its path. Where fear has gone there will be nothing. Only I will remain." This is a description of the landscape, calm and peaceful as the storm passes through: a description of me remaining calm and peaceful in the face of anger, hatred, violence, letting it pass through me and only I, at peace, remain.

Standing on the mall in the rain reminded me how wonderful rain is and how inappropriate it is for us to call the weather "bad" when it is raining. Ask a farmer in Oklahoma if a rainy day is a "bad" day. What would planet earth be like without rain? No trees, grass, plants, flowers, water—no life of any kind. Better that we should go outside when it's sunny and there are cloudless blue skies and look up and say, "Man, the weather sure is bad today."

I had the opportunity to put my new attitude about rain to the test a few nights later. When I first moved to Philadelphia I would often go out late at night and take a walk before going to bed. The streets were deserted, and I would usually end up at Front and Market streets, looking down (before I-95) to the Delaware River and the international tankers drifting by. This night I decided to see what deserted streets I could find in Chestnut Hill. I had no particular route in mind, so I took a detour to get an ice cream cone. I met some friends I hadn't seen in quite some time. We talked, but then it started to rain and so they left, and I walked on, expecting a brief shower. Before I had gone more than a few blocks it started to pour and within minutes I was soaked through to the skin. I had no choice at that point except to walk on, heading home, getting wetter and wetter, if that is possible, and feeling happier in the process.

Along the way I passed four teenagers—two boys, two girls—all soaked to the skin as well, carrying their shoes and walking barefoot. As we passed I said, "Great night, isn't it," and they said, "Yes, it's wonderful." I imagined them going home and telling their parents about the crazy old man walking in the rain, and I liked the idea of being thought of as a crazy old man who does things only teenagers would do. At the street corner I had to wait for cars to pass. The rain seemed to grow stronger. Something made me just stand there and raise my arms and face to the sky and the rain. Standing motionless, I felt as if the rain was God's nurturing love pouring down on me, cleansing and caressing my body. At the same time it felt as if it was cleansing my mind as well, washing away all my cares, fears, and worries. Yet it also felt that my body was a vessel being filled by the rainwater, being filled to overflowing by God's love. At that moment I was in complete harmony with God, in that "power of the Lord" George Fox often talks about, and life, *all* life, *my* life seemed extraordinary, wonderful, amazing, unimaginable, and blessed.

This is My Prayer

August 2000
Pendle Hill Pamphlet 358

When we began the vigil, we had one sign. It said, "Pray for Peace in Kosovo" because our concern was the NATO bombing. Over the past 16 months we have added others. They express our own individual way of sharing our thoughts about peace, and they provide opportunities for those who join us to select a sign that reflects a sentiment they want to share or perhaps one that speaks to their own condition. The signs all revolve around peace in different ways. "There is no way to Peace. Peace is the way." "Love your neighbor." "Disarm for peace."

I bring my own sign; it has changed from time to time, but within a very narrow range of expression. For a long time it was "Pray for peace in the world." Now it says: "Hear our Prayer: May there be peace everywhere on Earth." I made this one for the crowds we expected (and which showed up) around the Liberty Bell pavilion during the Republican Convention. It was influenced by the Peace Poles I saw in Dayton, Ohio, and in Richmond, Indiana, which contain the phrase "May peace prevail on Earth" in eight or ten different languages of the world. And it was influenced by Fred Small's song,

"Cranes Over Hiroshima," which contains the phrase "This is our cry, this is our prayer, peace in the world."

Whenever I have changed my sign I have found that it is important for me to include the word peace. After all, that is our purpose for our being there. But surprisingly, I have also found that it is important for me to include the word pray, or in this case, prayer. I know I do this because I want people to understand that we are not "protesters" (as that word is now used), that we are here for a spiritual reason. I know I do this because I want their response to be a spiritual one as well. But I often wonder what would happen if one of the passers-by came up to me and asked, How do I pray for peace? or How are you praying for peace while you stand here? I would be at a total loss; I would have to admit that I don't think I know how to pray.

My difficulty with prayer is influenced by my Catholic upbringing. As a child I was taught that prayer consisted of saying certain memorized verses while kneeling beside my bed before I went to sleep, the Lord's Prayer being the primary passage of choice. And I dutifully said it. Even now, in moments of stress, my mind and lips will often automatically recite it. But there were other kinds of prayers, too. My mother had a litany of saints to pray to, each for a specific purpose. Her favorite was St. Jude, the patron saint of lost causes. Whenever she lost something around the house she would pray to St. Jude and when it showed up (miraculously) she would regale us with the power of St. Jude's intervention. She had a natural faith that someone listened to her prayers and would answer them. I lost this, if I ever had it, when I became a Harvard-educated intellectual. There was a third kind of prayer I used most often as a child that I would call the conditional prayer. It took the form of "Dear God, if you let me pass that math test I'll be nice to my brother for a week." These prayers never seemed to work. Perhaps you can make such deals only with the devil.

When I became a Quaker and found that people used the phrase "hold in the light" rather than the word pray, I was greatly relieved. I felt I could relate to that, or at least to what I meant by holding in the light. I know that the "light" is God's grace, but imagine for the moment that it's actual light, a bright floodlight shining down to a circle of light on the stage. And imagine that the person you are concerned with is a miniature figure you can actually hold in the palm of your hand and that you take that person and literally "hold them in the light." The light gives clarity, warmth, optimism—many good things. But holding someone in the light means I am not asking God for anything. I am not asking God to make something happen that I have determined in my human (and all too often shortsighted) way to be the "right" thing for that person. I'm just holding them there. Basically, I'm saying two things: God, please be with this person, let them know that you are there and they can depend on you; and "Thy will be done." I am accepting for myself and asking support for that person to accept that whatever the outcome of the particular circumstance, it is good and part of a spiritual journey. If that is prayer, then that I understand.

I also understand Meister Eckhart's advice: If you can think of nothing to say, thank you is enough. I start my day saying thank you God for the gift of life and continue with thanks for the many gifts I have received. If that is prayer, that I also understand.

But when I read in books that one should pray, when people in my meeting say that they pray, I still feel lost. If one day that stranger approaches me on Independence Mall and asks me how to pray, how am I praying as I stand there, what will I say? Will I say that I am asking God to make Bill Clinton see the folly of a new missile defense system, or to make Bush and Gore see the wisdom of cutting the defense budget to zero, or to make the people shooting one another in more countries of the world than I can keep track of to stop? No, I do none of that. To me, for all the worthwhileness of it, that's just more of me, what I want, not a surrender to God.

In some sense I believe that my standing there is itself a form of prayer. I hope my mere peaceful presence says something to people. What I want it to say is this:

> *Please, go home and love your children, love your families. Love your neighbors. Don't be afraid of other people because they are different from you. Talk to them; work it out; be kind to one another.*

That doesn't sound like it will do much about world peace, does it? But then I am reminded of the Dalai

Lama's words: "Although attempting to bring about world peace through the internal transformation of individuals is difficult, it is the only way."

If each of us, individually, simply decided not to fight, not to let anger take over our hearts, to act always out of love and not out of fear or hate, then the world would be at peace. Isn't this all Jesus asked?

That is my prayer.

The Peace of God

December 2000
Pendle Hill Pamphlet 358

A YEAR AND A HALF AGO I started out seeking to do something to express my concern for peace in the world. Along the way I found a sense of personal peace I did not know I had. Reflecting on this experience has led me to consider the distinction between two kinds of peace: the peace of the world and the peace of God.

When someone comes up to me during the prayer vigil and asks about peace, I talk of the continued U.S. bombings of Iraq, the civil war in Sierra Leone, the fighting between Palestine and Israel. Peace is the absence of such events, a time when people are not fighting and killing one another. In these terms peace is external, something you can see and experience. Such a peace can be created by treaties, truces and ceasefires; by adequate defenses in a cold war. But such peace is fragile, easily broken or lost because there is no certainty that the underlying causes have been changed. This is the peace of the world.

The peace of God seems closer to what we mean when we use the phrase "inner peace." Recently I have been able to test my own level of inner peace, of how close I am to the peace of God. Several months ago I learned that I had prostate cancer. There is a point in the evaluation of prostate cancer when you learn you have it, but you don't know how advanced it is and whether it can be successfully treated or not. For me that period lasted about two weeks. While waiting for the test results I was looking for something in my journals and came across the entries I had written during a similar two-week period many years ago when I had taken my first blood test for AIDS and was waiting for the results. Those entries are filled with speculations about death, fear of death, descriptions of two weeks of nervous anticipation while I went about the normal events of my life in a state of inner terror. I can still recall my sense of relief when the test was negative.

By comparison, the two weeks between my prostate cancer test and the results were quite calm. There was a sense of inner peace that I did not have before, a sense of peace I still feel now. And so, I have wondered how this came about; what happened over the past ten years that has enabled me to handle a life-threatening illness so differently.

Buddhism has taught me that inner peace is not something you can seek. It is a byproduct, something that comes from a commitment to spiritual practice, in this case the practice of meditation. Peace comes as a result of learning to be detached, learning not to strive for things of the world for they are impermanent anyway. Although I do not know much about Islam, a book I am reading tells me that the word 'Muslim' means someone who has surrendered to God, and, it is implicitly understood, has found peace as a result. Some modern scholars use the word commitment instead of surrender. A Muslim's commitment to God is also reflected in a commitment to spiritual practice, in this case the practice of daily prayer and generosity. So, for a Muslim peace is also a byproduct of a spiritual commitment.

Where does my sense of peace come from? Most mornings I start my day with a form of Tai Chi I have adapted from one developed by Justin Stone. I call it Tree Energy Tai Chi because I do it with a tree as a partner. My first moves bend low to remind me that the root system of the tree extends unseen deep beneath the ground and prevent the tree from being blown over in heavy storms. My next moves extend upward to remind me that the branches of the tree are flexible so that the tree can adjust to the changing circumstances of wind and rain and snow. If the tree were not both grounded and flexible it could not survive the changing circumstances in which it lives. This is a good analogy for the way I feel. I am rooted, grounded in something deep and unseen that allows me to be flexible, to adjust to the storms passing through my life without being blown away or overwhelmed by them.

For me this grounding is an unequivocal trust in God. I trust that God is present in my life at all times, that God is guiding my life and in doing so is always acting for my good. It is this trust in God that brings me peace, not a peace that is merely neutral, an absence of desires or attachments, but a peace that permeates my body and fills me with joy and happiness.

Trust has come from a commitment I made ten years ago to turn the focus of my attention to God on a consistent basis without being certain what the results of that would be, or whether there would be any results at all. Once that commitment was made and my heart open to God, that was enough for God to come rushing in. My commitment to turn my focus to God began with the commitment to the spiritual practice of attending Quaker meeting for worship. Since then I have tried to turn my heart fully to God, to be open to whatever comes from that and to be willing to follow it faithfully. My trust is the result of an empirical process, of seeing God's presence in my life. I know with certainty that I am not separate from God, that God is with me at all times, and that God is always acting for my good, in a way that is appropriate to my spiritual life, whether I understand it or not. And it is that certainty, that trust, that has enabled me to rest in the peace of God.

At this time of year, may we remember the distinction between the two kinds of peace and renew our commitment to turn our hearts completely to God, for with that will come the peace of God, without which there will never be a true and lasting peace on earth.

April Fools

April 2001
Pendle Hill Pamphlet 358

LAST YEAR I wrote a report about what it had been like to hold the vigil alone for the first 10 or 15 minutes. On the first Sunday in April, I finally got to do the whole hour alone. At first I thought it was an April Fool's Day joke—my fellow vigilers staying away for a short period of time to make me think I'd have to be there by myself. But the combination of other commitments and the change in daylight-saving time actually kept everyone away for the entire hour.

Of course, I was not alone. I had two steadfast companions who remained with me the whole hour: members of the civil affairs unit of the Philadelphia Police Department who are now assigned to "guard" us and who sit in their car while we stand. I like to think that our message has become so powerful, and we have become so dangerous, that the police have to keep us under constant surveillance to be sure we don't somehow create a full-scale outbreak of world peace.

I recalled that last year in the short time I stood alone an African American woman paused and looked at our signs, then looked at me and said, "Bless you." She seemed a calm and peaceful woman. She wore a wooden cross on a string around her neck. Back then, I interpreted that phrase to mean something like, thank you for doing this and being such a good person—a compliment to me, if you will, a recognition of my spiritual goodness (though I know how inadequate my spiritual development truly is). Now I've come to think of that phrase, and the woman, in a different way.

A little book I picked up recently suggested that we start each day with a prayer asking God to give us a blessing. I start my day with a prayer giving thanks to God for the gifts I have received, which are many and varied. And I do ask God to help me to be an instrument of Its love that day. But I've never thought of that as asking for God's blessing. I realize now that the rote prayer I sometimes say at meals starts off with the phrase, "Bless us O Lord, and these thy gifts. . . ." And yet as often as I've mumbled that I've had no idea that I was asking for God's blessing or even what that might mean. Yet the idea has great power for me.

To receive a blessing is in a way to be anointed, to receive a transfer of grace from someone of greater spiritual accomplishment. For a Catholic to kneel before the Pope and ask for his blessing is a natural act. (Having been raised Catholic I know; I've done it myself, not to the Pope but at least to the archbishop of Boston.) A Buddhist might with equal ease do the same thing to the Dalai Lama. Each instance would be a humble acknowledgment of our lack of spiritual development in the presence of someone who has accomplished more, and a request that some of that accomplishment, some of the grace and strength that led to that accomplishment, pass to us. To be blessed is not, as I thought, a recognition of spiritual superiority, but in fact quite the opposite: the passing of spiritual strength and compassion from one who has it to one in need.

It seems quite reasonable for me to ask God for that as I start my day. Give me your blessing. Give me your blessing as I try to lead my life this day as a true member of your kingdom. Let me carry your love and compassion into the world and to all I meet. Recognize my inadequacies and go with me in this endeavor.

I think now that if I were standing alone on the mall and that African American woman gave me her blessing again, I would not stand there and nod my head as I did, seemingly acknowledging my spiritual goodness; I would put my sign down and go and kneel before her and ask her to place her hands on my head and give me her blessing, not just in words but with her whole being, knowing that it was she and not I who carried the spiritual strength. I might even kneel and bow in the eastern tradition or even go so far as to stretch myself out before her full length on the brick pavement until my forehead lay upon her feet letting her blessing, God's blessing, flow down upon me.

On Timothy McVeigh

June 2001
Friends Journal and Pendle Hill Pamphlet 358

OFTEN, I FIND that I cannot write a vigil report unless I can write something insightful, moving, something in which I both learn and share a new perspective on peace or prayer. But the truth is that not every Sunday at the vigil produces something that inspires me. Some days are boring and the time passes slowly. What I learn from these is an important fact: that part of being at peace is being able to live in and appreciate the present moment, whatever that moment might be. Living in the present moment is a strong part of Buddhist philosophy; it's a strong part of Jesus's too. Remember that man who filled his barns with grain and died that night? Lots of Jesus's sayings stress the idea that the kingdom is here, now, so live in it. And often by living in the present moment, incidents that seem boring and inconsequential to me at first blossom into something more. Here are a few of those apparently minor present moments.

Last Sunday, a man driving a horse-drawn carriage lifted his hand as he rode past to signal his support for us. He did it several times until I lifted mine back in acknowledgment. Shortly after that a young man walking with his friend on the far side of the street lifted his hand with two fingers extended, a sign for peace, and also did it repeatedly until I lifted my hand in acknowledgment. It's always a surprise to me to see who acknowledges us, among the many more who just walk by, heading for the bell, pretending that we are not there at all.

Several Sundays ago a man came up to me and asked questions. He had an accent I couldn't place and later told me he was from Italy. He asked who we were, and when he discovered we were Quakers he was surprised. He knew of Quakers in the 17th century and that they had left England for the New World, but apparently he lost track of them after that! So, he wanted to know the usual things, are Quakers Christian being the central question I usually get. But he said two things that stuck with me. First, he asked whether Quakers had power, power to influence public opinion, he said.

I glanced over my shoulder at the two other vigilers with me and almost laughed. Power? This meager group of three people have power? It seemed absurd. I almost laughed again thinking to myself, Quakers seek power? Oh no, not us. But when I answered I said that now and historically the power of Quakers to influence public opinion came from what we were doing on the mall—being willing to live our beliefs and bear public witness to them. He seemed satisfied with that and said that it was good that there was some group in the United States standing up for peace because the United States was not a force for peace in the world. To have peace, it is the U.S. that must change, he said.

These words reminded me of an interview I had seen on TV several weeks before. Mike Wallace asked (in an almost incredulous tone of voice) Jiang Zemin, president of China, whether he had actually said that the United States was the greatest threat to world peace. I wanted to shout at Wallace—how can you be so stupid! Isn't that obvious from our actions?! Jiang Zemin then proceed to give a calm and logical explanation why our high military budget, our arming other countries, our random bombings, our seeking a missile defense system—why all these things imperiled world peace. I was convinced.

Sometime around this same time I saw another interview on TV, Ed Bradley interviewing Timothy McVeigh. I confess I haven't followed our country's apparent blood-vengeance for Timothy McVeigh or heard many of his own statements. I watched the interview because it was there when I turned on the TV. Bradley asked McVeigh: Did he believe violence was the way to solve problems? McVeigh's answer was guarded and very carefully worded, as were all his answers. He said, "If our government is a teacher, if it models the behavior that it wants its citizens to follow, then the answer to that question must be yes." I was shocked to discover that I found this a very penetrating and accurate answer.

I have just finished reading the books *Conversations with God*, one and two. In one volume "God" says peace is possible: all that is required is that you all want it. That seems so simple. I tend to feel that if I asked any individual, "Do you want to live in peace?" the answer would be yes. Bosnian, Serb, Macedonian, Albanian,

Iraqi, Israeli, or Palestinian—all would answer yes. And yet when it comes to being the one to stand for peace, to unilaterally decide not to continue the violence, no one seems capable of doing it. Not even us, here in the United States, at peace in our own country, bombing Iraq every week for 11 years or maintaining economic sanctions against Cuba for, what is it, three decades? In the TV interview of Timothy McVeigh, one of the survivors said that the bombed federal building in Oklahoma city reminded her of images of Beirut. I thought of Baghdad. I have no idea what Baghdad looks like. But I imagine that it is a city in which there are a hundred bombed-out buildings like the federal building, each one the result of a bomb we have dropped. And so, I am forced to wonder about Timothy McVeigh: Is there a message in his madness?

These thoughts returned a week later when, on my way to Central Philadelphia Meeting, I happened to glance at the front page of the Sunday paper. There was an article that began with the headline, "Should we pray for Timothy McVeigh?" I carried this thought with me into meeting and it kept going around in my head. Finally, when I felt I had to speak, I decided to preface my remarks by saying that I had often heard it was not appropriate to base messages on what you read in the morning newspaper. As often happens in meetings, just before I was ready to rise a woman across the room stood and began her message by saying, " I have often heard it is not appropriate to base messages on the morning newspaper." She too had been struck by the same article and it led her to reflect on the nature of prayer, on the need to pray for those whose opinions were different from our own, and a reminder that whatever else prayer does it changes us.

As the meeting progressed, there were several other unrelated messages, but I found that my leading to speak had not gone away. And so, I was led to say something like the following: I too was moved by the article asking whether we should pray for Timothy McVeigh. When I first thought about it the answer seemed simple and obvious: of course we should pray for him. There is (was) that of God in him just as much as in me, his spirit will (has) gone to God at his death just as mine will. Of course we should pray for him and hold him in the light. But as I thought further I realized that I was not called to pray for Timothy McVeigh that morning. I was called to pray for myself, and perhaps for others in the room and in this country. For the past eleven years, every day of every week, the United States has bombed Iraq. Over that period of time, hundreds of thousands of men, woman, and children—civilians, just as innocent as the 168 people who died in Oklahoma City—have been killed in my name and I have remained silent. I have let it go on; I have not even written a letter to the president expressing my opposition. Timothy McVeigh has merely held up a mirror to my face and let me see what I have been doing. So, this morning I pray for my own forgiveness.

Dear God, please forgive me. Forgive me for my silence. Give me the strength and resolve to be silent and complicit no more.

Praying for One Another

June 2001
Friends Journal

IT WAS A SUNDAY this past February, only the second time I'd been at the vigil since early December, and the first time I was sufficiently recovered from my prostate surgery to feel well enough to be there. Nothing had changed in my absence. I saw the man on the bike I always saw ride by making a deliver, although it might have been another man, on the same bike doing the same task. The Independence Visitor Center under construction was now a skeleton of steel. If I inquired, I am sure I would have found that we were still dropping a few bombs on Iraq each week and more children had died as a result of economic sanctions. Nothing had changed.

Twice in the hour two young men yelled at us from a distance, somewhat angrily. I couldn't hear either clearly. The first said something about God and God's weakness; the second about our cause being worth as much as Jesus and that was nothing. Neither stopped—just rattled off their sentences without breaking stride both times. Perhaps I put my own words into their mouths. *Jesus stood for peace and look what happened to him*, was a phrase I thought of for the second man.

For the first, the thought was more complicated: *If God believed in peace why would God let all this killing go on? What makes you think that God will listen to your prayers? Just take a look at the world.*

A friend recently told me of a conversation she had with God. She asked why are people always getting killed in earthquakes and other disasters? She knew she was also asking why tragedy happened to others and not to her. God's answer, she said, was very clear. God shrugged his shoulders (if he would have had shoulders and been a he) and said, "I don't know." That seemed like the right answer to her, for her understanding of God, and the right one to me too. So yes, that guy was right: praying is in some way pointless. I don't expect God to intervene no matter how fervent our prayers, so why then do I carry this message, "pray for peace"?

I've wondered about this a lot since then. I'm coming to think that the act of praying doesn't really have anything to do with God. It has to do with us. When I pray, not very often I will confess, I am basically asking God to help me change—to pray for peace is to ask God to help me be a peaceful person and to take action to promote peace. It isn't asking God to do me a favor and straighten everything out. And what I'm praying for and asking for when I ask other people to pray is for all of us to change. I guess I'm praying for all the others, hoping that they will look into their hearts and repent, change their ways from hate and killing to love and helping. And asking everyone to pray for one another too. Because I imagine that if we were all on our knees sincerely praying for one another an hour a day every day it might change the way we lead the rest of our lives.

Grounded

August 2001
Pendle Hill Pamphlet 358

OVER THE MORE THAN two years I've attended the vigil, I've gradually learned to calm my mind for the hour I stand on the mall. Thoughts drift in and out like the clouds that drift by above me, but I am less distracted by them. I don't dwell on the things I have to do or rehash events that have annoyed me. I can watch people pass in and out of my field of vision without wondering where they are going or what they are doing or why they don't pay more attention to us. Sometimes I think about the connection between something I hear or see while I'm standing there and other aspects of my life, but more and more these reflections—the ones that find their way into these reports—occur late at night at home.

While I'm standing with my sign my mind is calm. I generally think this means that I'm at peace. But my body tells me this is not the case. It has a restless energy all its own that isn't connected to or influenced by the calmness in my head. And so, I shift my weight from one foot to another, bend my knees, turn my head from side to side or shift the position of my hands on the sign I hold—anything to help release this restless energy.

Last Sunday when I turned my head, I noticed Kaki doing her vigil in a seated meditation position on the ground. She looked far more relaxed than I did and seemed much more centered as well. It reminded me that earlier in the day I had passed by and seen a Chinese group in our usual place. While one woman handed out literature, two men and two women sat in the meditation position on straw mats. They too looked relaxed and centered and more at peace then I usually felt. This led me to reflect on how eastern religions seem to place a greater emphasis on the role of the body in spiritual practice. For a Buddhist, to be spiritually grounded is to be physically grounded as well.

I like the word "grounded." It conveys a sense of solidity and stability that words like "centered" and "focused" lack. It implies a connection to the ground, to the earth, and therefore to the natural environment, that has been an important part of my spiritual life and those moments when I feel I have really experienced the peace of God.

Recently I bought a copy of Loren Eiseley's book *The Immense Journey* because it was on sale for 25 cents. I'd read the book decades ago and loved it, but if you asked me what it was about I couldn't tell you. Eiseley is or was an anthropologist. What made the book distinctive for me was his ability to combine his scientific knowledge with a spiritual perspective. He reminded me of a statement I later heard about some contemporary astronomers, that the more they knew about the scientific reality of the universe the more they believed in God, in the existence of some divine, intelligent force behind it all.

One of Eiseley's essays has always remained with me. In it he describes going out into a mountain stream, lying down in the water and floating, letting the current carry him as it would carry a leaf. Because he is a scientist he can see himself in the context of a larger natural world. He can see, in his mind's eye, the great sweep of geography and himself in it as if he were an eagle soaring on the air currents far above the earth and looking down. He envisions the snow on the mountaintops melting and flowing down, collecting silt and sand as it forms streams like the one he is floating in, that extend into rivers that cross the continent and empty into the sea. Since he is a scientist, he knows his body is 70% water so he can imagine it both submerged in and merged with the water that carries him along, uniting him with it in an almost mystical way.

Many of my most extraordinary spiritual moments have come when I've felt a similar connection to the natural world, grounded, as it were, in a literal sense. One night I was lying in the grass on the hillside across the street from my house. It was late June or early July. Fireflies hovered a few feet above the grass all around me while others drifted up into the air under the trees that shielded me from streetlights and nearby houses. The sky was clear black and filled with stars. As I looked up I suddenly realized I could not tell which blinking lights were fireflies a few feet away and which were stars millions of light years away seeming to blink because of unseen clouds that passed between us. In that moment everything shifted: the lights close at hand might just as well have been the stars and I was there among them, my arms and legs spread out like a constellation. I could see myself in the context of the universe, small and insignificant, as I might have been seen by that eagle soaring somewhere far above. I was in the universe, but the universe was also in me; somehow I encompassed it all.

At that time, and in others like it, I have felt completely at peace, but a peace quite different from the one I normally know. It's not a peace like the calm mind and restless body kind of peace I feel while standing on the mall. Quite the opposite. My body is calm, entirely in its proper place, grounded, connected to and not separate from the natural world. And though my mind is calm as well, I am filled with an intense feeling of joy and happiness.

For me, true peace, the peace of God, comes when I relinquish my sense of independence and separateness and release myself into God's care. It comes when I am willing to lie in the grass, to float in the water, to crawl around on my hands and knees, and be a part of everything else and not a very important part at that—insignificant, powerless, and alone with God.

Being Faithful

July 2001
Pendle Hill Pamphlet 358

THIS MORNING the first speaker in meeting for worship reminded us that the theme of this year's Philadelphia Yearly Meeting was "faithfulness." She asked those who would not be attending, as well as those who would, to consider the meaning of this idea in our lives. The second speaker recalled a statement by one of the followers of Dorothy Day. When asked whether what he and Dorothy Day were doing through the Catholic Worker House to feed the poor was *effective*, he answered he didn't know whether he was being effective, but he knew he was being faithful.

This idea of being faithful immediately sent me into a downward spiral, leaving me feeling restless and disturbed. Several years ago our meeting adopted a practice of holding a separate meeting for worship with a visitor who came from time to time and who tended to be disruptive of our meeting for worship. Over a period of several years this worked quite well. I, along with one other member of the meeting, offered to be the points of contact for this process and so for several years I participated in these separate meetings almost whenever they occurred. Recently, I had asked to be released as one of the contact persons. When I arrived for meeting, I was told our visitor would be coming. As I sat in meeting for worship, I realized that this would be the first time in several years that I had not participated in the separate meeting for worship with him. I wondered if my decision not to do so was being faithful.

I knew that I had been faithful to my commitment to the meeting and that there was nothing wrong with being asked to be released. But what the messages forced me to consider was whether I was being faithful to myself and to God. I soon concluded that I had not released myself from this responsibility and knew I had to leave meeting for worship and join the other group. And so I left. In the other group I found myself more at ease, more open to listening and looking with love at the other participants. And I realized that the act of being faithful is an individual calling; what being faithful meant for me—to join this other meeting—was not necessarily what others were called to do and that was fine.

After meeting, the idea of faithfulness challenged me again. It was a beautiful day. The sky was beautifully blue, filled with huge white clouds; it was warm but there was a pleasant breeze. I thought how restful and peaceful it would be to take a walk along the Wissahickon Creek, to lie in the grass beneath the trees and listen to the water flowing. In comparison, I thought of attending the prayer vigil for peace. I would have to drive on the expressway into Center City, stand in the hot sun, on hard pavement, endure the droning noise of constantly passing buses and the indifferent stares of people walking past. Those of us who attend the vigil often miss a Sunday from time to time; I've done that myself. To skip a day would have been no big deal, I felt. But the question of faithfulness would not go away, nor would it allow me to accept an easy out: I'd been called to do this and so must go.

As it turns out I was there alone for a while and only one other person joined me. With only two of us I felt my decision to come had been the right one. As I stood there I wondered per usual about the point of our actions. Were we being effective? I recalled a story I read some time ago although I can't remember where or remember the story exactly. It goes something like this: A bird is sitting on the branch of a tree in winter. A bird-friend comes by and asks what the first bird is doing. He says, I am counting the number of snowflakes it takes to break this branch of the tree. Impossible, his bird friend said; snowflakes weigh nothing, they dissolve in your hand, you are wasting your time. But the first bird kept counting and as he counted the 1,347,519th snowflake to land the branch broke. As the bird flew away, it left its friend with a message that could easily be adapted to our situation: Who is to know whether it is you or I or a person that we meet who, upon deciding to make a commitment to peace, becomes that one final person needed to break the branch of war and violence in the world.

This reminded me of the first vigil report I'd written almost two years ago. In that I compared the parable of the sower to my actions on the mall. He didn't know which seeds would grow; I don't know which of the people who pass will go away changed and increase the possibility of peace. It's easy to get discouraged. Sometimes I feel like the one millionth snowflake and that neither my actions nor those of others working for peace have any impact. But most of the time I find that I feel optimistic and full of joy from knowing that I am, at these moments, acting in harmony with God, doing what is asked of me. Dorothy Day's friend had the answer for me. I no longer wonder if I am being effective, if I've thrown enough seeds or if the next snowflake, next person who flashes me a thumbs up, will be the one to finally ensure peace. That's not my task. Thomas Merton reminds me that "The real hope is not in something we think we can do, but in God who is making something good out of our work in some way we cannot see and cannot know about beforehand."

Our task is just to be faithful; God will do the rest.

Shepherds in the Fields

December 2001

ON CHRISTMAS EVE night, I went out to find the closest thing to a field within walking distance of my house so that I could see what it might have been like to be a shepherd. The field I found was across the street. It's a baseball field in summer, a soccer field in fall, but this time of year the ground is hard, and the grass is low, much like I would imagine a field suitable for grazing sheep would be. The night was cold, and the moisture on the grass glistened as it turned to frost.

The field is surrounded on three sides by houses and tall trees, but the other side is open, and when I walk there, I tend to face in that direction. This night I saw Orion, that great Greek man, lying on his side and high above his head I saw a very bright star. A star too bright to be a star, a planet most likely, Jupiter or Saturn. That made me think about the wise men and wonder if that is what they saw too. But then I know the Arabs were great astronomers and would not have been so easily fooled. The shepherds must have seen the star too, and as I looked up at it, so bright in the night sky, I realized I was facing east toward Bethlehem.

I don't know much about shepherds. I know they were looked down on by the Jewish society because their lifestyle prevented them from following the required religious customs. Undoubtedly, they could not observe the Sabbath, nor could they follow all the dietary and sanitary restrictions. I imagine their nomadic life prevented them from marrying and having families, as was the expected social norm. Perhaps they chose that life deliberately; perhaps they were men like me, who preferred the company of other men and were willing to live in the social margins to be able to find that opportunity.

The best picture I have seen of the shepherds on this night is by the painter Carl Bloch. It shows about half a dozen men in the fields, and in their midst, in the center of the picture, is an extraordinary light. Within the light the outlines of a figure can be seen, but so faintly as to be barely visible. All that is there is an intensely bright light, too bright for human eyes to look on directly, and so the shepherds have thrown up their hands to shield their eyes or have even turned their heads away. Three shepherds are looking out of a lean-to tent; they have robes or blankets wrapped around their waists, but their upper bodies are naked as if they had been sleeping, wrapped in one another's arms. Others lie on the ground or kneel nearby. Their faces are startled, reflecting the story's words that they were much afraid.

This night in the field, I wondered what that might have been like. I tried to imagine a bright light before me, brighter than any star I could see, as bright as the sun come down to rest ten feet in front of me, a light too bright for human eyes and a voice out of nowhere. Would I have been one of the shepherds to rush off to town to see the child the voice spoke of, or would I have stayed behind with the sheep, as someone must have had to do? They went, saw a child, came back to their fields, told the ones who had remained behind what they had seen, and went on with their lives. Did that one look change the way they lived? Were they more peaceful, more loving towards one another; did it sustain them for the next 30 years when nothing happened and nothing seemed to change?

Though I have gone to the Sunday peace vigil for the past months, I haven't been inclined to write about them. I've wondered about that. It is as if I have been silenced and what has silenced me is not the events of September 11th but those of October 7th, the start of the bombing of Afghanistan, and thereafter. I don't want to write because I don't want to feel what I feel, and that is a deep and profound sense of hopelessness. Nothing I can say to myself, nothing I've written about faith and God, can shake off the feeling that peace will never come. And yet, each Sunday I show up.

I came to the vigil last Sunday after spending the day with a young man from Germany working at a Jewish community center as an alternative to serving in the military. The night before we had been out with a friend of his who is here doing the same thing. They are both 20 years old. They have a sense of the history of the effects of war that I will never have, and it has given them a passionate commitment to peace. Their sense of history leads them to understand that we are all human, that differences are inconsequential, and so they have a passionate commitment to equality as well. I see these same attitudes in my sons. I look at all of them and am grateful to see how much the world has changed in the 40 years that have elapsed since I was their age.

At the vigil, it was very crowded. People wandered all around us waiting in line for the Liberty Bell or pressing their noses against the glass. Four young men, also in their twenties, came up and asked if they could each take a button (we had made buttons that said, "Peace be with you" and were giving them away). They put them on, wished us good luck, and walked away. A girl of ten or so came out of line to take four buttons for her family. I saw her sister take one, but her parents shook their heads, and she returned theirs. All the children that came near were prepared to pin the words "Peace be with you" to their coats without the slightest hesitation.

My Christmas card this year contains a quotation mistakenly attributed to Oscar Romero. It begins with the phrase, "The Kingdom of God is not only beyond our efforts, it is beyond our vision," and goes on to say that no matter how hard we try to carry out God's work, we may never see the end results. "That is the difference between the master builder and the worker. We are workers, not master builders. We are the prophets of a future not our own."

Sometimes, it is necessary to take the long view and have faith that God's work is being accomplished even if we can't actually see that. The children who took the buttons, my young German friends, were for me that day the long view, that view of a future not my own, a future in which I could believe not only that peace was possible but would be. And I could readily imagine that the shepherds saw that too in the face of the child they went to see and returned to the fields believing that the words that came to them out of the light would come true, that there would be peace on earth and goodwill toward all people.

A Thief in the Night

February 2003

For a long time now, it has seemed that each Sunday afternoon has been dark. Either it has snowed or been overcast or so cold that I focus my attention down at the ground, merely trying to keep warm. I may glance up from time to time to look at people, but my eyes seldom go higher than that, and when they do, all I can see is a gray and overcast sky.

On this day, my attention was suddenly caught by bright sunlight reflected off the edge of the Constitution Center and the U.S. Mint. As soon as I saw it, I realized I hadn't seen sunlight there in a long time. The light made me look higher, and I saw lots of gray clouds moving eastward across the sky. At their edges and in between them, I saw the pale blue sky emerging. Soon the dark clouds were replaced by whiter ones with more blue sky surrounding and showing through them. It was almost a theatrical moment, a moment when the light comes beaming through, symbolizing a change from something sad or difficult to something good and joyful. The first thought that came to my mind was, "peace is here." Not just there where we stood but here on earth, everywhere. Something seemed different, as if at the moment when the blue sky and bright light returned, people's hearts all over the world looked up and changed.

How will peace come? Not with trumpets blaring, not with the sounds of fireworks and whistles, not with parades and marches or politicians cheering. Peace will slip in silently when no one is looking—like a "thief in the night," I think the phrase is. We will all feel joyful without at first knowing why or what has changed. And when we look around, it will be like looking up at the sudden blue sky and bright sunlight but what we will see is God's inner light shining forth from the faces of everyone we meet.

A Song of Peace

April 2003

DURING MEETING FOR WORSHIP this morning, I heard several people question the relevance of the signs they still had in their yard: "Peace is patriotic" and "No War on Iraq." I wondered about the signs we hold at the vigil, particularly the one I have been holding. I thought it said "Pray for peace with Iraq" as a statement of my hope that we would reach peace before we went to war. But when I checked my sign, I realized it said, "Pray for peace *in* Iraq." That still seemed relevant, so I held on to it. But the distinction was subtle, and one passerby reminded us that that we were irrelevant, at least in his view, with his comment: "It's over."

Today our "Peace be with you" buttons flew off the table. There were lots of people around despite the added restrictions around Independence Hall and the Liberty Bell. Many groups seemed to include lots of teenagers and young adults as well as young children with parents. I particularly remember one young boy who walked by, then came back with his mother pointing out to her the buttons on our table. I went up and asked him if we would like one. He said "yes" and pinned it on his jacket. He was wearing a military-style green jacket with Air Force insignia all over it. A large shield on his back said, "Fight." As I watched him walk away, I smiled, wondering if he was aware of the inconsistency of his messages.

It seemed right to be there today. The number of people who took buttons told me that there were lots who didn't think it was over, that peace had not finally prevailed on earth, and many needed encouragement to preserve their commitment to peace. I seemed to reach a decision without knowing I was trying to make one that I would continue to stand here in the months ahead. Perhaps it is the warm weather that encouraged me to consider doing so, but whatever the reason, it seemed like the right decision.

The sky in front of us was clear and blue, and as I stood, I found myself humming a song I'd just heard for the first time. It sums up a great deal of what I am feeling these days. The music comes from a section of Sibelius's *Finlandia* to which someone else added words around 1932. It goes like this (you'll have to hum the tune yourself):

A Song of Peace

This is my song, O God of all the nations;
A song of peace for lands afar and mine.
This is my home, the country where my heart is,
Here are my hopes, my dreams, my holy shrines.
But other hearts in other lands are beating
With hopes and dreams as true and high as mine.

A Song of Peace

My country's skies are bluer than the ocean,
  And sunlight beams on cloverleaf and pine.
But other lands have sunlight too and clover,
  And skies are everywhere as blue as mine.

O hear my song, thou God of all the nations,
  A song of peace for their land and for mine.

Thinking Ahead

March 2004

It's March, but I look ahead to April, the month of my birth. When April comes, God willing, I will have completed the 64th year of my life and the fifth year of the prayer vigil for peace on Independence Mall. The 64th year isn't a particularly significant landmark, just a reminder that my life is two-thirds over (again, God willing) and that I need to figure out what I am doing with what's left. But the end of the fifth year of the vigil is a different issue: it requires me to stop and ask myself if I am continuing and, if so, why, and of course, if not, why not.

When people ask me why I started attending the vigil, the answer is simple and easy to give: God asked me to. Sometimes I word that differently, saying I was led or called to do it, which is often easier for people to hear since there is something in saying "God asked me" that can sound arrogant or presumptuous as if I were an Old Testament prophet to whom God speaks directly in clear and uncertain terms. Hardly. It's often a challenge to discern God's leadings, but this one was fairly easy. Over the years, I've read a lot about discerning leadings, and I think I've done reasonably well in discerning the ones that came to me. Of course, I could be totally wrong. Often, I wonder if these things that seemed to me to be so clearly leadings of the Spirit might not merely be temptations of the devil, designed to lead me into good works and away from a truer calling. Good works, the feeling that one is doing good for others, can easily be a temptation in itself.

But discerning when I am led to do something, if my decisions have been approximately right, has always been easier than discerning when I am led to stop. There is a Quaker story of two women in the colonies who felt led to travel to England to preach the word of the Lord. They prayed and presumably counseled with their meeting, concluded the leading was a true one, and prevailed upon a ship captain to take them to England. Halfway across the Atlantic, they looked at one another and realized that they were no longer led; they had 'been released' is the proper phrase, I think. And they bid the captain turn the ship about and take them home. Whether he did or not, there likely being other passengers involved, I do not know. Perhaps their leading was just a test of faith—were they prepared to up and leave home and family to follow God's will, a sort of mini-version of Abraham's call to take Isaac to the mountaintop. The issue was not accomplishing what was asked; the issue was whether you were willing to do what was asked, and setting sail across the ocean was proof enough of faithfulness; there was no need to actually arrive and preach. How did they know they were released? The story doesn't tell me that, nor do other things I have read.

Sometimes there is a natural ending to things and it's clear when a leading should be laid down. But many of the things I got into from spiritual motivation are still with me, or I with them. It's hard to say, "that's all, it's time to move on," because that seems to be my own judgment. Rarely is there a message as clear and strong as the one that got me started. The messages that get me started more often than not come to me from others. I think of them as God's messengers who come to me in strange ways and ask something, say something, or suggest something that is understandable in ordinary human language, but beneath which only I hear God's voice: "This is where I need you now," it says. And so I go. But seldom does the messenger appear and say stop.

For many years the vigil was a strong source of spiritual growth. It added something to my spiritual practice quite different from attending meeting for worship or from my other activities. It forced me to think about peace and prayer in a way I hadn't done before, and those thoughts found their way into written form because I was inspired to share them with others. For more than two years now that has not been the case. I still enjoy my hour on the mall, people still respond in interesting ways to our presence, but the activity doesn't speak to me in the way it did before. I'm rarely inspired to write about the experience either for public consumption or for private reflection in my journals. Yes, this period corresponds to the period after September 11th (no one will ever need to give the year), and is, in some respects, a reflection of my ambiguity about what a person of peace does in this world, in this country I guess I should say, that finds violence so easy a solution to its problems. I know I don't have the answer to that, and I am no longer sure that my mere standing with my sign is answer enough.

And so, I wonder, what will April bring?

There is Another Way

May 2004

ON SUNDAY, most people who passed by our vigil and spoke made a simple comment. Generally, they just said "I agree with that" in response to our signs that say such things as "Peace for Everyone." This commitment or desire for peace transcended the differences of the people who passed—race, country of origin, male/female, and I am sure religious backgrounds made no difference. But early in the hour, one woman who stopped for a button said something different: She said, "I believe in prayer." Although some of our signs say pray for peace and our action is a prayer vigil, I was, nonetheless, surprised to find someone who focused explicitly on prayer rather than on peace. Near the end of the day, a group of women stopped and approached our table to take buttons. One said to her friends, "you should start each day with prayer; your whole day should be a walking prayer." I liked that thought—a walking prayer. It reminded me of Fox's advice: *Be patterns, be examples and walk cheerfully over the world answering to that of God in everyone you meet.* He might have put it more simply and said, "Be a walking prayer."

Across the street, in the area of the mall set aside for

public events, there had been a larger gathering earlier in the day complete with stage, sound system, music, and speakers, including Bono, the lead singer of the band U2, one of my favorites. He was participating in an event for a cause in which he has taken a significant interest, that of AIDS and poverty in Africa. I didn't attend the event, and so I have no idea how many it attracted. But as I watched the workmen take down the stage, I thought about how many worthwhile causes there are and how easy it is, in many respects, to attract people to them. Sometimes the attraction is just the event—being with other people who share your views about something. But more than that I think the attraction is that perhaps you can do something about it, you can change the situation by getting involved. And no doubt people can and do; Margaret Mead said something to the effect that all great movements start with a few individuals.

But these thoughts reminded me of a statement of Thomas Merton's to which I referred in a vigil report several years ago. "Do not depend on the hope of results," Merton wrote in this letter. "It's not what we achieve but how we allow God to act through us." For Merton, the elimination of AIDs and poverty or the establishment of peace are the results we seek through human action. They may or may not come, and even if they do come, there will still be a list of other causes requiring our attention. This doesn't mean we shouldn't try to do something about these situations, but it does mean that addressing AIDS in Africa, for example, is, in many respects, addressing the symptom and not the disease (if I can use that analogy).

Prayer is not a result; it is something else—a process, perhaps. It is a process of listening to God and allowing God to act through us; a process of letting God determine the appropriate results; a process of surrendering to God; a process of trying to act in harmony with God in all things; a process of believing that with God all things are possible and without God nothing lasting can be achieved; a process of trying to change ourselves. To believe in peace is, in fact, relatively easy. It's a tangible state we can all agree is worthwhile, even if we have difficulty agreeing on the way to get there. To believe in prayer is much more difficult. To commit oneself to such a process is much more difficult. But committing to that process, to the goal of changing oneself, to the goal of acting in harmony with God in all situations—to be, if you will, a walking prayer—is the only way that has the potential to address the underlying cause of all issues that distress us. That underlying cause is our lack of real and tangible compassion for one another. No, not just for one another but for everyone—for every one another.

I watched the men loading the stage and sound equipment onto their trucks. Two of them often stood and looked our way in between their tasks. What are they thinking, I wondered? Did they compare our small silent group of nine with the loud crowd of hundreds that most likely were there to hear Bono speak and think how ineffective our actions were in comparison?

Or did they stop and stare because our signs made them stop and think about another way of achieving change? I don't know. But it is the possibility of the latter that compels me to return each week.

Independence Day Blues

July 2005

On July 4th, Independence Day, five people gathered for the vigil on Independence Mall. We were surrounded by hundreds of visitors, milling about and heading for the Liberty Bell pavilion or the Visitors Center. There were American flags everywhere you looked: many people carried small flags, others wore t-shirts with flags on them. Outside the Liberty Bell pavilion, long lines of people waited to get in, the first time I've observed that all summer.

Behind us on the grass was the American Friends Service Committee (AFSC) exhibit of pairs of shoes, each one with the name of one of the 800 American soldiers who have died in Iraq. I was surprised how little space this display took up—not more than a quarter of the grassed area in the center block of the mall—and consequently, how insignificant the display looked. Yes, that was my reaction: insignificant. How many were dead in Vietnam before the numbers became significant enough to change American policy? Was it 50,000? We have a long way to go, I thought, before the dead will bring an end to the American occupation of Iraq. And "only" 800 dead in a war that has cost billions of dollars and has overthrown the government of another nation is a remarkable achievement.

It disappointed me that AFSC had bought into the government's public relations message that only American dead count—Iraqi civilian deaths aren't worth counting. How much more astounding it would have been to see some sign of the 10,000 Iraqi civilians who have been killed since the war "ended." What symbol might have brought that home? Children's and women's shoes, perhaps. I once saw a photograph of a similar exhibit about the Israeli/Palestinian conflict in which the dead of one were represented by white coffins and the dead of the other by black. The collection filled a huge public space wherever it was that the exhibit was held. It made a much more relevant statement to me than this collection of black boots. I don't mean to be harsh; I regret their deaths all the more so because so unnecessary. But let's be realistic, too.

Many people came by us who had visited the exhibit. They wore the old AFSC pin that says, "No War On Iraq." How strange, I thought; that cause is lost. Is there no current message? That seemed to symbolize the situation. What is our message? What is mine?

Farewell Flyby

September 2005

TODAY AT THE VIGIL, three fighter jets flew by so low that the sound of their jet engines was loud enough it made me look up and follow their path as they headed south. For a moment, I could imagine what the people of Iraq must feel each day, except in their case, the noise of the planes is undoubtedly followed by the noise of bombs falling and exploding.

I assumed the jets were headed to the stadium for a flyby over the football game, but I could be wrong. In my imagination, I humorously thought they might be there for me, a farewell flyby in honor of my diligence over the past five years and my decision to retire (if you can call it that). But then, that would be unlikely. More likely, the flyby was a reminder that though I might go, they—the planes of war—were still there and would continue to be. Peace has not prevailed.

At the Movies

REFLECTIONS ON THE TESTIMONY OF HONESTY/INTEGRITY

January 2010
Friends Journal

IN 1952, ERNESTO GUEVARA DE LA SERNA set off on a journey with his friend Alberto Granado. They traveled by motorcycle from Buenos Aires, where they lived, to the northern tip of South America in Venezuela. Their journey and adventures are portrayed in the movie *The Motorcycle Diaries*, adapted from Ernesto's travel journal of the same name first published in 1993 and then again in 2003.

In the movie a narrator's voice reads Ernesto's words from the travel journal. Near the beginning the narrator recites the opening lines of the journal: "This is not a story of heroic feats. . . . It is a glimpse of two lives running parallel for a time, with similar hopes and convergent dreams."

The idea of two lives running parallel is an appropriate analogy, for Ernesto and Alberto share a journey in common, but each has his own individual journey as well—influenced by their individual objectives for the trip and their personalities.

Alberto's goals are clear: He wants to reach the tip of the continent on his 30th birthday and to have sex with women in each country, perhaps even each town, through which they pass. He is outgoing, gregarious, full of humor and a great dancer. He charms, or tries to charm, everyone he meets. But his charm is a form of manipulation—to get sex, food, or a place to stay. He tries to ingratiate himself with everyone, but he has no interest in anyone once he has achieved or failed to achieve one of his three objectives. As a consequence, Alberto makes few real connections on the trip. He is essentially the same person at the end of the journey that he was at the beginning.

Ernesto's goals for the trip are less clear. He says to a couple they meet on the road, "We travel to travel," and that seems to sum up his objectives. The trip is a break from his medical studies and a chance to see South America. Ernesto, five years younger than Alberto, is shy, serious, somewhat introverted, insecure with women, and a terrible dancer. His personality is formed by a significant defining characteristic.

Early in their travels, Ernesto and Alberto come upon an isolated house in the woods adjacent to a mountain lake. An elderly couple live in the house. When the man finds out that they are doctors—a not-quite-true fact (Ernesto is still a medical student and Alberto is a biochemist) they use to help gain support on their travels— he asks them to look at a lump on his neck. Alberto glances at it and says it's just a cyst, nothing significant, and could they have some food and a place to stay.

Ernesto fingers the lump carefully and says it's a tumor and the man should get to Buenos Aires as quickly as possible. Afterwards Alberto complains, "The trouble with you is you're too honest." The statement implies that Alberto was already aware of this characteristic of Ernesto's and recognizes it as the critical difference between them.

Ernesto's honesty and Alberto's manipulative charm are shown in scene after scene. Their tent gets blown away in a rainstorm and they need a place to spend the night. They approach a ranch house, and the rancher comes to the door. He is sullen and asks what they want. Alberto tells a long story of how they are medical doctors traveling across the continent trying to find the cure for an incurable disease. He is charming, or so he thinks, and obsequious, but the rough-mannered rancher will have none of it. "What do you really want?" he asks angrily. Ernesto replies in a simple straightforward way: We need a place to stay. The man says he does not like Alberto, but Ernesto he likes so they can stay in the barn with the field hands.

Later, they stay with a doctor who invites them into his home, shows them around his hospital and arranges for their passage to a leper colony in Peru they wish to visit. In return the doctor asks them as a favor to read his novel, the secret passion of his life. Of course, both agree to do so. As they are about to get on the boat to go to the leper colony, he asks what they thought of the novel. Alberto in his obsequious manner says, "No one writes like you do"—leaving it unclear to the viewer and doctor alike whether he has even read the book. Ernesto looks serious and then replies that the novel is terrible, that it is unreadable, and the doctor should stick to what he knows best, medicine. For a moment there is a silence as the doctor stares at him. Then he shakes his hand and says, "Damn you, boy, nobody's been this honest with me. You're the only one."

Telling the truth was George Fox's first spiritual decision. It was, you might say, the ground on which his future spiritual life was based. In the opening pages of his journal, Fox describes how at the age of eleven he was led to make a commitment to telling the truth at all times. "For the Lord showed me that though the people of the world have mouths full of deceit and changeable words, yet I was to keep to yea and nay in all things," a reference to the phrase "let your nay be nay and your yea be yea" in the gospel. Telling the truth at all times was Fox's first step toward a spiritual life.

Truth-telling, honesty, was the first Quaker testimony, a commitment expected of all persons who joined Fox's religious society, which was first known as the Publishers of Truth or Friends of Truth. Honesty really means consistency: responding the same way to everyone all the time. For Quaker merchants this meant charging the same price for their goods to all people, rich and poor alike, a practice not common at the time. Honesty, consistency, means telling the truth at all times (therefore there is no need to take an oath to that effect in a court of law, a practice that caused Quakers great difficulty in English courts).

Honesty says something about ourselves, but it also says something about our attitude toward other people. Alberto sees others as instruments merely to be used to achieve his purposes of food, shelter, and sex. Ernesto sees other people as people with lives and needs of their own. Honesty is a sign of respect for the other. Although Ernesto's truth-telling seems to be a conscious decision regarding honesty, by telling the truth he conveys his respect to all the people he meets. As a consequence, he connects deeply and personally with people at a human level and people respond to him in the same way. Honesty and mutual respect open Ernesto's heart to the suffering of others and to a feeling of compassion, a visible compassion that grows as his journey progresses.

Compassion is concern translated into action, not just an emotion or feeling. On the road at night they meet a couple traveling to find work. They have lost their land because they are communists. Ernesto's compassion is evident in his face as they talk by a campfire. He gives the woman a blanket to keep herself warm. Later we find out that he gave them the fifteen American dollars his girlfriend had given him to buy her a bikini if they reached Miami—money he had steadfastly refused to give Alberto, even when they needed food or Ernesto was ill and needed hospital care.

Ernesto stares at peasants riding in a boat tied to the back of the more comfortable boat in which he rides. He stops and talks to a man who has been thrown off his land. The plight of people moves him. "Let the world change you," a quotation of his says at the start of the movie, "and you can change the world." He is open to the world and it changes him, makes him compassionate, and his compassion leads to generosity. Ernesto has nothing, but he gives everything he has; he gives away his life to everyone he meets.

In a small town they meet two sisters. It appears that one of their fantasies is to have sex with sisters. They charm them—even Ernesto charms them. As they are about to head off with the sisters for a tour of the village, one of the workers who has heard that they are doctors asks Ernesto if he will come see his ailing mother. Of course, Ernesto says yes. While Alberto goes off with the girls, eventually to one of their beds, Ernesto sits by the mother's bed trying to comfort her, conveying the sense that he knows there is nothing he can really do. He gives the woman a bottle of pills, which one suspects is his own asthma medicine.

He never gets the girl—not the girl back home whom he loves, not the girl on the boat, not the woman in the dance hall, not one of the sisters: none. Alberto gets them all. But it is Ernesto who leaves a trail of love behind by giving his life away, over and over again.

Honesty, respect for others, compassion, generosity: These traits are most fully expressed when Ernesto and Alberto visit the leper colony. Although leprosy is not contagious when under treatment, the nuns who staff the colony require everyone visiting the section where the lepers live, on the opposite side of the river from where the healthy staff live, to wear rubber gloves. Ernesto politely refuses (and Alberto follows). This small gesture creates a different relationship, an honest relationship, between him and the patients. His compassion shows as he sits by the bed of a woman talking with her about his own illness, trying to ease her pain. At the colony his generosity is that of the spirit—he gives himself to the patients fully and without reservation. After celebrating his birthday with the staff on the "well" side of the river, he cannot bear to not have the patients be part of the celebration, too. So, in the absence of a boat, he swims the river in the middle of the night to be with them on the other side.

At the end of the trip, while they are at the airport preparing to go their separate ways, Alberto to a leprosarium in Venezuela and Ernesto back to Buenos Aires to finish medical school, Ernesto says: "Wandering around our America has changed me more than I thought. I am not me anymore. At least I am not the same me as I was." He has become aware of the discrepancies between rich and poor, something he had not come into direct contact with before while leading a comfortable middle-class life with his family and as a medical student. While he may have begun his journey with a rigorous commitment to telling the truth, he has ended it with qualities of compassion and generosity that he did not have before, which in turn will nurture the sense of social justice that will emerge in the coming years.

Today the Quaker testimony of honesty is often referred to as integrity. Integrity is a big and complicated word. It certainly includes telling the truth, but telling the truth is a relatively simple matter—each of us knows when we are doing it and when we are not, even if it's only a "white lie" we may be telling. Integrity means a larger commitment to being true to your values in all things, not just in telling the truth. And so, it requires a clear understanding of these broader values, a clear incorporation of them into one's personality so that all actions are consistent with those values. Ernesto always told the truth, and we might be inclined to say that because of that he was a person with integrity. But it is not likely he would have said that of himself at that point in his life, living as he did a comfortable middle-class life that ignored the inequities around him and even, to some degree, benefitted from them. Nor would George Fox have referred to himself as a man of integrity at age eleven when he started telling the truth at all times; for him, too, that would come later.

An interesting insight on the meaning of integrity is given in another movie, *Moonstruck*. The story revolves around four characters—a mother and father, their daughter, and the brother of her fiancé. One evening the mother goes out to dinner alone because her husband and daughter are out. Unbeknownst to her, and to each other, her husband is attending the opera with his mistress and the daughter is attending the same opera with the brother of her fiancé—with whom she has just had a sexual encounter. The mother invites a man to have dinner with her after he has had an incident in the restaurant with a younger woman he had apparently been dating. The man tries to be charming and later walks her home. When they reach her house the man asks if he can come in, but she answers no. Although the house is empty, she says she is a married woman and then she gives her real reason: she says, "I know who I am."

It is easy to understand that she means she knows what her values are. She is clear that she is a woman who is faithful to the commitment she has made to her husband. The key factor is not what her husband or daughter might think if they found out she had a sexual encounter with this man; the key factor is what she thinks about herself. She is a woman who sticks to her values whether others are aware of this or not. Her statement, *I know who I am*, implies not only an understanding of her values, but that she is also clear how they influence her actions. She is not tempted, because that is not the person she is. To be a person of integrity is to not only to have a clear set of values, but also to act in accordance with them at all times.

But the statement "I know who I am" goes beyond an understanding of values and actions. It is also a statement about identity. Identity goes much deeper than just knowing one's values. It means that those values have been so incorporated into one's character that they are no longer a matter of debate or discussion; they are automatic, without thinking or ambiguity. They are not "second nature," as we often say; they are first nature, performed without hesitancy, instinctively, without even thought.

What does it take to reach a point where you can say with confidence "I know who I am"? Ernesto's and George Fox's experiences suggest that it comes after a long practice of telling the truth at all times, even when it might seem uncomfortable to oneself or others. The development of a broad set of moral values that is the basis of integrity comes later. But the development of those broader values—whether you call them ethical, as Ernesto might have, or spiritual, as Fox would have been inclined to say—begins with what seems to be a simple act of merely telling the truth.

Can you say that you are always honest, that you always tell the truth—rigorously honest, not just when it's easy and convenient or required, not even telling the occasional white lie, the veiled response like Alberto's "no one writes the way you do"? I know that I am not. I often tell a lie for convenience; if a friend asks me out to dinner and I really don't feel like it I might say I have another engagement or some work to do. This response seems harmless to me, but I know it is a lie and I know as soon as I utter it that this is not the person I want to be. I know it is disrespectful to my friend to believe that our friendship is not strong enough to sustain my telling the truth.

Ernesto's physical journey began in Buenos Aires and took him over 8,000 miles across the continent to the northern tip of Venezuela; his spiritual journey began at the same time, taking him from his commitment to honesty to one of compassion and generosity and eventually becoming a life-changing commitment to social justice. My spiritual journey, your spiritual journey, can begin now or begin anew if we are prepared to follow Ernesto's and Fox's example to tell the truth at all times, in all circumstances and to all people.

On Love

December 2011
Friends Journal

THE GREEK LANGUAGE has four words for the one English word "love:" *storge*, meaning love of family; *eros*, meaning romantic or sexual love; *philia*, meaning brotherly love or friendship; and *agape*. *Agape* is the word used throughout the gospels when Jesus refers to love. It is generally defined as an unconditional, boundless love for all creation. Many people feel this is the essence of his teaching—that we should love one another unconditionally. While this may be true, Jesus's conception of love and what it means to love one another is quite different from the normal understanding of that word. For him, love has a more tangible and practical meaning as can be seen from the statements and stories in which the word is used.

Jesus's most well-known and most challenging statement about love is, "Love your enemies, . . . do good to them that hate you." (Matthew 5:44) This statement provides a definition of love that is consistent throughout the gospels. The structure of the first half and the second half of the sentence is the same, making it clear that the word love means to do good. Interchanging the words—do good to your enemies, love those who hate you—doesn't alter the meaning of the sentence in any way.

Love, therefore, is not a feeling or an emotion: it is an action, a positive action directed toward another person. This is not to say that there aren't other forms of love that involve feelings and emotions; there are, but that is not the challenging idea of love presented in this and other statements. The fact that we are directed to do good to our enemies—knowing that we are naturally inclined to do good to our friends—makes it clear that the willingness to love, to do good, is not influenced by the person who is the recipient. We extend good deeds to friend and foe alike. This idea is well put in the *Hua Hu Ching*, a Taoist text attributed to Lao Tzu. It says:

> *The first practice is that of undiscriminating virtue: take care of those who are deserving and also equally take care of those who are not.*

The fact that we are advised to do good to others regardless of who they are suggests that the inclination to do good comes from our own character, from the nature of who we are. It is similar to the Buddhist concept of "loving-kindness"—a desire for the well-being of others that comes from the heart and is demonstrated in visible acts. The ability to do good and to extend loving-kindness comes from within; it is the result of an inner change that is manifested in our behavior toward others. Neale Donald Walsch puts this in an interesting way:

> *When you decide ahead of time that your inner state of being is going to be peaceful, understanding, compassionate, sharing, and forgiving no matter what the outer moment brings, then the outer moment has no power over you.*

Doing good to our enemies because that is the nature of who we are also suggests that we do so without expecting anything in return. The fact that we are willing to do good does not provide assurance that our enemies will be willing to do the same for us. Our actions may not change their feelings or behavior at all; that is fine and irrelevant. To do good to your enemy is to do so because you want to, because that is the nature of who you are and not because you are expecting to gain anything in return or even that you expect your actions to have an influence on your enemy's actions. Perhaps they will over time, but that is not the guiding motivation.

The idea that love is an action is also reflected in the story of Jesus's conversation with Peter at the end of the gospel of John. He asks Peter, "Lovest thou me?" (John 21:15) using the word *agape*, meaning "do you love me in a boundless, all-encompassing way." When Peter responds, he uses the word *philia* as if to say, *I am your friend; of course I like you.* Jesus repeats his question and Peter responds in the same way, each using a different word for love. When Jesus asks for the third time, he uses the word *philia*. It almost seems as if he realizes he has tried and failed to make Peter understand the larger dimension he means by the word "love" and so has given up trying. However, after each time Peter answers—even after the last—Jesus says, "Feed (or tend) my sheep." He seems to be suggesting that even to love only as a friend is still an action; show that you love me by taking care of the poor and marginal members of society to whom my teachings have been addressed.

Jesus gives a further indication of what he means by love with the phrase "Love one another as I have loved you." (John 13:34) This phrase forces us to look at Jesus's relationship to his disciples and ask what it meant for him to love them, that is, to do good in relation to them. The most vivid and radical expression of his love is described in the gospel of John's version of the last supper. (John 13:4–10) After they have finished their meal, Jesus removes his robes, wraps a towel around his waist, and begins to wash his disciples' feet. Peter objects, but Jesus says that if Peter is truly to be one of his followers, he must allow his feet to be washed. He does and Jesus proceeds to wash all the rest, including the feet of Judas.

In this case to do good is defined as serving another. Jesus takes the lowly position of a servant, kneeling on the floor and doing a menial task. Elsewhere he frequently talks about the need to be willing to be a servant: "If any man desires to be first, the same shall be last of all and servant of all." (Mark 9:15) Here love is not simply doing a good deed, it is serving the needs of another—a positive action that puts another's needs first.

The idea of putting the needs of another first is found in other spiritual traditions as well. One of my favorite examples is a Muslim story told by al-Ghazali. Two Muslim men are preparing to start a journey. One says to the other (I am paraphrasing), *This journey will be difficult, and we will only be successful if one of us leads. It does not matter to me if you or I lead, so you decide.* The second man thinks this over and concludes that allowing the other to lead will be a generous act and will earn him good favor in the eyes of God. So, he says, "You lead." At that, the first man goes over and picks up the other man's pack as well as his own. "What are you doing?" the second says. The response is, "You said I should lead." When they reach camp for the night it is raining so the first man sits outside in the rain holding a stick to support a cover over his sleeping friend. And so it goes throughout the journey, illustrating the first man's willingness to be servant of all, to show love and do good by putting the other man's needs ahead of his own. Service to others is the highest good, the truest expression of love.

The phrase "Greater love hath no man than this, that he would lay down his life for his friends" (John 15:13) often seems to me to be misunderstood. For many the phrase "lay down one's life" is thought to mean a willingness to die. This hardly seems consistent with the overall character of Jesus's teachings, which celebrate life. For me "lay down your life" means to be willing to set the direction and activities of your own life aside for a while in order to assist another person move ahead with his or her life. A servant puts another's needs first, ahead of his own. He stops whatever he may be doing when called upon for assistance. A friend who does good for another does the same—she sets aside her own interests, the activities she is currently engaged in, and even puts the direction of her life on hold temporarily in order to help another. The definition of love offered by the psychologist M. Scott Peck captures this idea well. He says:

> *Love is the will to extend oneself for the purpose of nurturing one's own or another person's spiritual growth.*

At one point Jesus points out that the Jewish law says, "Love God with all your heart and love your neighbor as yourself." He goes on to say (I paraphrase again) "How can you say you are following the law when your brother has filthy clothes and is hungry and you have a fine house and nice possessions?" The implication is clearly that if you truly loved your neighbor you would be doing good by sharing your resources with others less fortunate. Once again love is an action, a positive action that goes beyond merely giving assistance to include sharing your resources as well.

Although the parable of the Good Samaritan is given as a response to the question "who is my neighbor," it provides a compelling illustration of the practical application of all these ideas about the meaning of love. The story is familiar enough not to need repeating. If we look at it step by step as an illustration of what it means to love this is what it shows.

The Samaritan comes across a man in need. Although the story does not identify him as Jewish, everyone who hears this story—both now and, I imagine, then—assumes the man to be Jewish. Thus, the Samaritan helps—does good for—someone he knows hates him, someone who sees him as an enemy and someone he may see as an enemy, too.

The Samaritan cleans his wounds, gives him clothes, puts him on the donkey and takes him to the inn. In providing this assistance the Samaritan is serving the needs of the other man. He lays aside his own life—that is, he delays whatever journey he is on himself, he takes a side-trip to the inn that he wasn't planning on making, and he gives over the day he expected to spend traveling to assist the man.

The Samaritan pays the man's expenses at the inn. Thus, not only does he do good by sharing his time and his abilities in caring for the man, but he also shares his resources with someone in need, someone who at the time at least is less fortunate.

Lastly, the Samaritan does all these things without expecting anything in return. He continues on his journey without leaving his name and he may or may not believe that the Jewish man, his enemy, would thank him—that is irrelevant to him and not a motivation for his actions.

Thus, the Samaritan consistently acts from his own inner conviction that helping others to the fullest extent he can is the right thing to do, regardless of who they are.

When William Penn said, "Let us then try what love will do," he did not sit at home and think fond thoughts about the Native American population of his colony. He put his beliefs into action: He went out and signed a treaty with them that respected their interests and established a basis for peaceful co-existence between colonists and Native Americans that lasted for seventy-five years. He took a positive action and did good to people who were at least strangers, if not enemies.

So, the next time you hear yourself using the word love, think of what it truly means. Understand that it is not simply a nice feeling or an emotion, but concrete, practical action as illustrated by the parable of the Good Samaritan and summarized quite succinctly in the *Hua Hu Ching*:

> *To practice virtue* [to do good, that is, to love] *is to selflessly offer assistance to others, giving without limitation one's time, abilities and possessions in service whenever and wherever needed, without prejudice concerning the identity of those in need.*

Then, try to follow the advice given to Nicodemus, the man to whom the parable of the Good Samaritan was told: "Go thou and do likewise."

Holy Saturday Meditation

April 2015
Friends Journal

It is holy saturday, the day between Good Friday and Easter Sunday, the day on which nothing happens. For me, this day has always been the most important day of the year. It is a day on which, far more than any other, faith is tested. Jesus is dead; what happens next is unknown and uncertain.

Right after the 3PM Good Friday service, the Catholic churches I used to attend would strip the altar of all the flowers, vestments, candles, and other paraphernalia that was usually there. The door to the tabernacle would be left open showing that it was empty, that there was nothing there. No candles would be lit. The church I remember best had gray stone columns and walls, so the few lights left on cast a dull gray pallor throughout the interior. The atmosphere suggested death, absence, a certain barrenness I found more comforting than when the church was fully illuminated and filled with colorful robes and ornaments. I used to go there late on Friday or Saturday night, when the dull gray light was more in keeping with the darkness outside, and ponder the open tabernacle much as I imagine those who came on that Sunday morning might have pondered the open tomb. Was he a man or was he the Son of God? Did he just die or was he indeed resurrected? These were the questions I asked. I did not have answers then; I do not have answers now. My intellectual side has prevented me from making the leap of faith even though in my heart I might want to.

There are no services on Holy Saturday because, as I said, it is a day on which nothing happens. I have often wondered what the disciples did on that day. The Gospels tell us that most ran away after Jesus was arrested in the garden, fearing they too might be the subject of arrest. Only Peter and John tried to follow Jesus to see what would become of him. Peter goes to the palace of the high priest to try to find out what is happening. He tries to hide himself among the servants, but he is discovered, accused, and denies three times his knowledge of the man he said he loved. He wanders away in despair not to be heard of again until the third day. Judas, the betrayer, drifts away eventually to his death.

John, we are told, is able to infiltrate himself among the temple priests and witness the trial before Pilate and the crucifixion, something none of the others can know about because they have disappeared and presumably gone into hiding. I can imagine the first one making his way in the early morning light out to Bethany on the outskirts of Jerusalem, the place where they had been staying, and sneaking stealthily into a barn. Here he hides, waiting. When he hears someone else entering he is cautious, as is the man entering, both afraid of being caught by the Roman soldiers they imagine are searching for them. But then, recognizing one another, they embrace in relief and share their fear and their lack of knowledge. Slowly, throughout the day the others show up, one by one. Having found their separate hiding places in the night, they now return to where they think the others might return also. What happened to him? they ask one another. I don't know, each says. I heard the shouting of the crowds, that's all I know.

When John arrives, he tells his story, without recriminations for their abandoning Jesus, without knowing of Peter's denials until he shares them, sorrowfully, with the group. John tells of the public portions of the trial, of Jesus's demeanor, of the priests' accusations and Pilate's judgment. He tells of the journey to Calvary, finding Mary Magdalene and the other Mary along the way, the time on the cross and the last words, the anguished *"O God, why hast thou forsaken me?"* He is shaken by the experience, his story interrupted by periods of crying in which the others join. He tells of the final moments, of lifting the body down from the cross, carrying it to a nearby cave, wrapping it in a shroud and rolling a stone in front to seal the entrance until a proper place of burial can be found.

Perhaps there are some who remind the others that Jesus said he would rise from the dead. Perhaps there are some who do not believe this, who do not know what to believe and doubt—much like Thomas, who will need hard evidence to be convinced. Perhaps they debate the issue and, in spite of their fear and the feeling that they should leave the city as quickly as possible, they decide to stay and see what happens. What other choice do they have? They are lost, all seems lost, and the way forward is unclear if there is a way forward at all.

The day wears on. Finally, the women who returned with John come bringing food and drink from the house. They share their story; they share their sorrow. They hear the disciples' uncertainty and share it. Let us at least go to the tomb tomorrow morning, they say, and anoint his body properly and then we can try to move it to a more suitable burial place. But, one disciple says, he raised Lazarus from the dead, why could he not raise himself? Silence follows. The question remains unanswered.

At night they pile together in groups of two or three in different corners of the room and sleep. It is a restless sleep, a sleep disturbed by the uncertainty of their safety as well as the uncertainty of their future.

In the morning, Peter and John are awoken by the cries of one of the women. "Come," she shouts; "he is risen." They get up quickly, others join them awoken by the commotion and as a group they rush out the door to follow the woman back to the tomb. Only one remains, Philip perhaps, so deep in sleep that he is undisturbed by the cries or commotion. After the others have left, leaving the barn door flung open, he wakes. He turns beneath his blanket and looks around at the empty room, wondering what has happened and where everyone has gone. He gets up and wanders aimlessly around the room while stretching his body, naked except for the loose loincloth around his waist. The early morning sunlight streams through the open door and across the floor. He walks into it. He feels the sun on his naked skin, feels its warmth, and he senses in that moment what it is to be truly alive. He lifts himself on his toes, arms extended upward, fists clenched as if in triumph and shouts a passionate Yes!

There is no need to know what happens at the tomb. There is no need to know whether there was a resurrection or not. There is no need to see the risen man, no need to place your hand in the wound in his side, no need to meet him on the road. The true resurrection, as Philip will later tell us, happens in a different way for those who hear his words and follow them.

> Those who say that the Lord died
> and then was resurrected are wrong;
> for he was first resurrected and then died.
>
> If someone has not first been resurrected
> they can only die.
> But if they have already been resurrected
> they are Alive as God is Alive.
>
> You must awaken while in this body,
> for everything exists in it.
> You must resurrect while in this life.

At the Movies 2

REFLECTIONS ON LEADINGS AND SPIRITUAL JOURNEYS

May 2016

At the beginning of the movie, *Field of Dreams*, Ray Kinsella introduces himself and gives a brief overview of his life to date. He begins by telling us that his father wanted to be a baseball player, but when he couldn't make it out of the minor leagues he gave up and took a job he hated at the Brooklyn Navy Yard. His hero was Shoeless Joe Jackson, a member of the Chicago White Sox team that was banned from baseball for having thrown the 1919 World Series. Ray and his father frequently argued about Shoeless Joe, among other things, which led Ray to move to California for college so that he could get as far away from his father as possible.

Ray describes himself as a child of the '60s. While in college he engaged in the typical activities of a college student of that time and met a woman from Iowa who would become his wife. Now, in his mid-30s and many years after his father has died, Ray finds himself married, with a daughter, living on a farm in Iowa. Up to this point, he says, he has never done a crazy thing in his whole life.

Although no one in the movie mentions God or says anything that could be considered spiritual, *Field of Dreams* is a spiritually inspiring movie. Most people would say—taking a clue from the title—that it is about following your dream no matter how far-fetched it might seem. But from a Quaker perspective, the movie is a remarkably clear illustration of what it means to follow a "leading" and the implication of seeing life as a spiritual journey.

Following a leading is a particularly Quaker concept, although other spiritual disciplines refer to something similar when they use the word "calling." To be called and to be led both imply following a particular direction or path in response to a spiritual motivation. Although the two have much in common there are, at least to me, significant differences. A calling usually refers to following a specific way of life or career: Thomas Merton felt called to be a monk; Dorothy Day felt called to serve the poor; other people speak of being called to be a teacher or to support specific social causes. In this sense a calling is something that may be felt only once or perhaps twice in a lifetime and have a long and lasting influence.

Leadings on the other hand can occur frequently and are usually short-lived. John Woolman had a leading to visit Native Americans. Unlike his concern for slavery, it was not something that he pursued throughout his entire life. Paul Lacey uses Woolman's example to offer a definition of leadings and being led:

> [A true leading] ***begins inwardly*** *as a process or motion of caring whose direction and object are* ***unclear,*** *so a*

> *time of waiting must occur, during which time Woolman rigorously examines himself, learns his limitations and frailties but also his strengths and achieves **patience and perseverance**. From that patient waiting a concern arises and becomes clarified and directed and **leads to actions on behalf of others**. (emphasis added)*

My own definition draws on similar ideas but is slightly different: a leading is an unexpected, divinely inspired and strongly felt inner urge to do something that you would not normally do about something that concerns you without knowing what the result of your actions will be. *Field of Dreams* illustrates this well.

While working in his cornfield, Ray hears a voice. He is startled and believes it is a person hiding somewhere among the cornstalks. But no one is there, just a voice that says, "If you build it, he will come." For Ray, hearing a voice is certainly unexpected, something out of the blue, and what it suggests that he do is vague and unclear. To help him determine what this means, Ray decides to consult with friends, in this case his fellow farmers. He asks if they have ever heard voices in their fields and gets a lot of good-natured kidding in return, but no answers.

The memory of the voice and the feeling that it is asking him to do something persist and Ray struggles to determine what it means with a growing sense of frustration in much the same way that Woolman undoubtedly struggled with his leading to visit the Native Americans. Then, one night, Ray has a vision of a baseball field in his cornfield, complete with floodlights, and of Shoeless

Joe. He shares his experience of hearing the voice and this vision with a more sympathetic audience, his wife, thereby testing his leading a second time. When he says he feels compelled to build this ball field so Shoeless Joe can return, he asks her, "Am I crazy?" "Yes, you are," she says; "but if you feel so strongly that this is something you should do then do it."

The key word for Ray, the key word for leadings, is "compelled"—compelled to do it even though it seems crazy, even though it is totally contrary to your normal way of life, even though you really don't know why you feel compelled or what the outcome will be. There is no rational way to explain it; you simply have to trust your feelings, the same type of feelings that you may have when the spirit moves you to speak in a meeting for worship.

Ray builds his field and for a year nothing happens. Fall becomes winter, snow covers the ground, then spring returns. One night, while Ray and his wife are reviewing their dire financial situation, his daughter says, "There are men on your lawn." And sure enough Shoeless Joe appears, followed by his White Sox teammates. Dead baseball players come back to life and interact with Ray and his family as if they were real people themselves. "Are you real?" Ray's daughter asks Shoeless Joe. When he responds, "What do you think?" she says, "You look real to me."

One might think that Ray's story should end at this point: he has followed his leading, built his field and Shoeless Joe has come back. His task is done, and he can get back to his normal life. This is usually the pattern with most Quaker leadings I have read or heard about or experienced myself. But Ray's story doesn't end here. Once again Paul Lacey helps to frame Ray's experience:

> *If we are not open to leadings, we will be less able to know them when they come. But even if we are obedient, we will not always know where we are to go or how far. Our sight will come to us as we go. We will be able to see the way only as it opens. The consequences will be out of our hands and perhaps will never seem to have borne fruit, but that will not matter because we will know that we did what we were called to do, to follow our lead.*

And so it is with Ray: his willingness to follow his first leading leads to two others whose meaning is equally unclear, but whose direction Ray is willing to follow without knowing where he is being led.

The second message from the voice says, "Ease his pain." With the help of two coincidences, Ray concludes that this means he should go to Boston and find Terrance Mann, a writer he admired in the '60s, and take him to a Boston Red Sox baseball game at Fenway Park. The two coincidences are a controversial discussion of Mann's books at his daughter's school and a dream his wife has about Fenway Park. Although the movie doesn't use the word "coincidence"—and several more appear later in the film—it implicitly suggests that such events are not accidental or meaningless, but deliberate signposts that help Ray find his way once he has made the commitment to follow his leadings no matter how crazy they seem. In a certain sense, the confirmation of the truth of his leadings is that "way opens" as he follows them.

While at the game with Terrance Mann he hears the voice a third time—"Go the distance," it says—and sees the name "Archie Graham," a former baseball player, on the Fenway Park scoreboard. These two events lead him and Mann to go to Minnesota to find Graham. But when they arrive, they find that Doc Graham, as he is known to the local townspeople, has been dead for sixteen years. Discouraged and confused, Ray and Mann start back to Iowa. Along the way they pick up a young man who says he wants to be a baseball player and is looking for a place to play. His name, he says, is Archie Graham.

On the way back to Iowa, Ray mentions to Mann the source of his personal pain. He spoke angrily to his father when he left and, as Ray puts it, "the son of a bitch died before I could take it back." This is the burden he carries, the one regret he seems to have about his life. His remark is so casual it almost seems insignificant. However, once back in Iowa, late one afternoon as the ballplayers are leaving for the day, Shoeless Joe repeats to Ray the first words of the voice: "If you build it, he will come." As he speaks, he looks in the direction of home plate where the catcher is taking off his mask and chest protector. Ray recognizes his father as he was as a young man when he played in the minor leagues. He now understands that the "he" was not Shoeless Joe at all. He sees his father in that moment not as the tired old man Ray knew—the one who hated his job and his life and tried to pass on his love of baseball to his son—but as a young man with hopes and dreams and ambitions. They play a game of catch in the fading light of the day enabling Ray to express his love for his father and feel his father's love for him.

And here, it seems to me, the movie captures in a very moving and inspiring way the essential and often overlooked aspect of a leading: while leadings may seem to be about an external issue or person and the actions we are encouraged to take directed to and of benefit to that issue or person, the true significance of following a leading is that it takes us on a journey the real purpose of which is our own spiritual growth. While in the end it may be unclear what our actions have accomplished, we ourselves are changed: we are a different person than we were at the start, farther along our spiritual path and closer to God by virtue of having been willing to surrender control of our life and to follow a leading no matter how crazy it seemed.

And so it is for Ray. He may have followed his leadings for the benefit of others—for Shoeless Joe initially, then for Terrance Mann, then Archie Graham, and then for his father—to enable each of them to complete some aspect of their spiritual journey. But in the end Ray is not the same person he was at the beginning either. He has restored the bond of love with his father and lifted the burden of regret he has carried for many years; he has achieved a new "wholeness" for himself and is ready now to lead a fuller life. What that will be, how the experience of following these leadings will influence Ray's future spiritual journey, we do not know. We only know that at the end of the movie there is a long line of cars in the night heading for the flood-lit field, carrying people who may also see dead men playing baseball and as a result have their dreams restored, hearts softened, love rekindled and find inspiration to continue their own spiritual journeys.

While Ray's story is about following a leading, Archie Graham's brief story illustrates an important aspect of seeing life as a spiritual journey. Archie's dream was to be a baseball player. But when learning he was to be sent back to the minor league after his one inning and no chance to bat in the majors, he goes home and becomes a doctor, as was his father. When Ray and Terrance Mann find that he has been dead for sixteen years they also learn that he was much beloved by his community. Ray goes out in the evening for a walk and finds himself transported back to 1972. He meets Doc Graham who tells him of his frustration at never having had a chance to bat. But when Ray offers him the opportunity to come along and join the White Sox on his field, Doc Graham says no; "My place is here." Not to have been a doctor, he says, would have been the real tragedy.

As the young Archie Graham who Ray picks up on the way home, he does get to bat and hits a sacrifice fly driving in a run. Shortly after, Ray's daughter falls off the bleachers and seems to be hurt. Ray looks imploringly at Archie, who comes to the edge of the field where he hesitates for only a second before he steps off and the magic is over: once off the field he is old Doc Graham again and is able to remove the hot dog stuck in Ray's daughter's throat.

Archie's story suggests that sometimes the path we think we most desire for ourselves is not the path God has in mind for us. On a spiritual journey some doors may have to close in order for other doors to open. For Archie, the closing of the door to a baseball career opens the door to a much richer and more rewarding life, a life of compassionate and loving service that left a lasting impact on all the people in his community.

The willingness to follow leadings and the ability to see life as a spiritual journey may very well lead us to experiences or life-long paths we would not have chosen ourselves. The key is to be open to the unexpected—whether it takes the form of a compelling inner urge or an undesired external event—and to be willing to embrace fully the path to which we are led without knowing where it will take us.

Sisyphus

November 2019

For part of the year I live in Niantic, Connecticut. When I am there, I begin each day with a walk along the boardwalk that stretches for about a mile along the edge of Niantic Bay. I start at the west end and walk east; consequently the early morning sun shines directly in my eyes. Its reflection off the water is bright, too bright to look at for more than a few seconds at a time. There is also usually a morning breeze blowing in my face as well. Both factors make the walk physically difficult; I keep my head down, struggling against the elements, focusing on the concrete deck of the boardwalk while trying to be alert to other walkers, of which, fortunately, there are usually few. My attention is entirely focused on the physical effort of walking. If I am aware of anything at all it is only sound: the sound of the waves breaking on the rocks, the gulls screeching overhead, or the whoosh of the Amtrak train racing by.

By contrast, on my way back the wind is behind me, as is the sun which brightly illuminates the boardwalk and the distant vista ahead. I can lift my head and gaze out at the vast expanse of water and sky, at the curving boardwalk ending a mile away in a small stretch of sand—Hole in the Wall Beach—with McCook Park rising on the hill beyond. I can see the spire of St. Agnes Church, hear the bells ringing on the hour, see the tops of houses, and watch the flight of gulls gently floating down to rest on the water or the rocks. The world I see, glowing in the morning light, is beautiful to behold. In those moments, I am fully present to the world around me.

The walk reminds me of the Greek myth of Sisyphus and Albert Camus' essay of the same name. For a transgression of excessive pride, Sisyphus has been sent to hell, condemned to the eternal task of pushing a heavy boulder up a hill only to watch it immediately roll down again once it has reached the top. Both the myth and the way it is generally discussed focus on the pointless, futile, and frustrating task of pushing the heavy boulder. Camus, on the other hand, draws attention to Sisyphus as he walks back down the hill momentarily free of his chore in what he calls "the hour of consciousness." He is what Camus calls an "absurd" man because he knowingly says yes to the absurdity of life.

> *At each of those moments when he leaves the heights and gradually sinks toward the lair of the Gods, he is superior to his fate. He is stronger than his rock. . . . One must imagine Sisyphus happy.*

In my imagination, Sisyphus stands at the top of the hill and laughs as the rock rolls down again. His laughter is an expression of his pleasure in the absurdity of it all, of which he is fully conscious. On the walk down, he can lift his head as I lifted mine coming back along the boardwalk; he can see whatever landscape existed in the Greek understanding of hell. He can even remember the view of the sky, sunlight, and trees that he had seen on earth from similar hillsides. His gaze could fall on whatever activities surrounded him. In those few moments, he is free, free to live in that present moment and enjoy it to the fullest. The gods may control his body and force him to push the boulder endlessly up the hill, but they don't control his mind. If going up the hill there is the physical pleasure of the body pushing the rock, then going down there is the pleasure of the mind—the freedom to contemplate not just the world, but life itself.

Unlike Sisyphus, my walk comes to an end. When it does, I sit on a rock near the edge of the water, mesmerized by the steady sound of small waves breaking on the sand. The sunlight glitters on the surface of the waves, a flickering silver light of great intensity, almost like individual pieces of light that dance on the water. The waves come steadily one after another, but none are large enough to attract surfers, not even at high tide, or even sufficient to support a brief run on a belly board. The bay is calm, a wide expanse of gentle undulations stretching out to the horizon. The beach is covered with broken shells a few feet from the water's edge, followed by soft sand on which no one lies these days for it is now November. But if it weren't for the wind, the sun is still warm enough that it would be possible to lay there in just a bathing suit and be comfortable.

I count one hundred waves, a form of meditation, then hear the church bells telling me it's time to get about my day. There are still boulders to be pushed. But the walk back, much like Sisyphus's walk down the hill, has rejuvenated me, inspired me, and made me happy and willing to take up the task again, as I imagine it did for him. If by chance he was successful in getting the rock to balance at the top, to allow him to sit for a moment to contemplate the view as I contemplate the waves, I have no doubt he would soon give it a gentle nudge sending it down the hill to start the process all over again. For what pleasure would there be in the walk down if it were not in contrast to the effort of the walk up?

Camus says the myth is tragic because Sisyphus is consciously aware that he cannot succeed but continues his efforts anyhow. It is this perseverance in the face of a lack of hope that makes him an absurd hero. Hope is the refusal to accept life as it is right now, to believe that there is something more desirable than the present. Sisyphus tells us that it is acceptance without hope that brings happiness.

Holding in the Light

March 2020

When the Covid-19 pandemic forced me into isolation in March 2020, I begin holding what I referred to as a solitary meeting for worship on Sunday morning at the time I would usually attend Quaker meeting for worship. Since I was meeting alone, there was no opportunity to offer a message if I felt led to share one. Therefore, I decided to write short reflections on my experience and share them with other Friends, similar to what I had done many years ago during the prayer vigil for peace.

Meeting for worship by myself provided a space for thoughts and feelings to rise to the surface in a way quite different than when worshiping with others; it was an unexpected gift.

W<small>HEN I SIT DOWN</small> for meeting for worship on First-day morning, alone in my apartment, the first thing I do after settling into a period of silence is to visualize the meeting room in which I would be seated in normal times—when there is no pandemic to prevent us from gathering. I visualize the room filled with the people who usually attend each week and slowly look around the room, bringing to mind each individual I imagine

I see. This is relatively easy as most people sit in the same place each week. As my inner eye moves around the room, passing from one set of benches to the next, I silently say the name of each person as I see them come into view. On the way, I'll come to a spot where an occasional visitor sits who often delivers a message I find annoying, and I include him in the group as well because today I want to pray for him, too. I might even throw in a few unknown people representing the visitors who frequently come to worship with us, some attending a Quaker meeting for the first time.

It is easier for me to imagine all these people in their regular places in the meeting room than to try to imagine them one by one scattered throughout Philadelphia in their own houses or apartments. Once I have them all assembled, as it were, my natural desire is to pray for their well-being in this complicated time. But then I ask myself, what does "to pray" mean for a Quaker? Traditionally we say, "I'll hold you in the Light" rather than "I'll pray for you." I'm comfortable with that phrase, and it is full of meaning for me.

Recently I read an interview given many years ago by Rabbi Harold Kushner, author of the well-known book *When Bad Things Happen to Good People.* He expressed his ideas about prayer in a very Quakerly way. He said, "When I pray with someone who is in the hospital, we are not praying for a miracle cure or a good outcome to surgery. We are praying for the presence of God." Of himself, he said, "Presence is the essence of prayer . . . I don't pray for specifics. I simply and openly pray for the presence of God because I am a different person when I feel that I am in the presence of God." God's job, he says, "is not to make sick people healthy. That is the doctor's job. God's job is to make sick people brave."

That is what I mean—and what I think Quakers in general mean—when I say, "I'm holding you in the Light." I am praying that you can feel God's presence in whatever circumstance you find yourself, and that feeling the presence of God will give you the courage and strength you need. When I do this, I actually try to envision a bright light encompassing you, almost like an aura emanating from your body as if that Inner Light we believe is present in all of us has burst forth and now envelops you externally as well as still shining brightly within.

At the same time, I am acknowledging that I don't know what the best outcome for you is, and you may not know that either; we both may have to surrender our desire to control the situation and accept whatever outcome God has in mind. But that doesn't mean sitting passively by and expecting God to do all the work. It means having the courage to face our situation and take the best actions we can to address it, knowing that the outcome may not be in our hands.

When asked by a follower whether he should tie up his camel when he got to the oasis or trust God to look after it, Muhammad (peace and blessings be upon him) said, "Trust in God, but tie up your camel." We must each do our part as best we can and trust that God will take care of the rest.

Entering the Stream

April 2020
Pendle Hill Pamphlet 469

My only visible companion for today's solitary meeting for worship is Buddha. I know there are other less visible companions here too—God, Jesus, and Quaker friends in solitary meetings in their own homes and apartments. But Buddha is the only one I can see; he is here in the form of a statue on the bookcase opposite where I am sitting.

Buddha is seated calmly and peacefully as he always is, observing silence with me. But his silence is different from mine. He is not waiting for anything, or perhaps I should say he is waiting for "nothingness"—for that state of pure being, free from all thought and desire. On the other hand, I am waiting for an inspiring message to help me along my spiritual journey. In meeting for worship, such messages almost always originate with something outside myself—from something another person says that resonates with something deep within me and calls forth a response, or from the sound of birds chirping or a passerby singing. Or from an event—the unexpected appearance of a friend or the presence of a stranger visiting for the first time. They are all God's messengers, whether they know it or not, sent to tell me something I need to know, or to share, to help me or another on our way.

My statue of Buddha cannot speak, but its mere presence makes me wonder what Buddha might say to me today if he were the one to bring me a message. I am reminded of a passage I read recently in Thoreau's journals that has a Buddhist connection. Thoreau wrote, "If one would reflect, let him embark on some placid stream, and float with the current." He discusses the difference between the hard labor of trying to paddle your boat upstream against the current with the "sublime, but ever calm" experience of merely allowing the boat to drift downstream. He talks in terms of his boat, but I think of it in terms of my body: wading into a cool mountain stream, turning on my back, and floating peacefully like a leaf on the surface of the water.

In Buddhism, a concept called "entering the stream" uses the physical struggle against or the surrender to the stream as an analogy for the spiritual journey. You can try to impose your will on life, or you can accept the events and experiences that come along and allow yourself to be carried forth by them without being concerned where they will take you. "Happiness or sorrow—whatever befalls you, walk on untouched, unattached," Buddha says. Acceptance without judgment—to see things simply as they *are* and respond appropriately—this is the message he brings me, and I think it was Jesus's, too.

Two days ago, I observed my eightieth birthday. As I reflected on these many wonderful years, I realized that little of what has happened to me, of what I've done or experienced, has been the result of my own decisions. My life has not been under my own control. Just as the messages that come to me in meeting for worship originate with messengers outside myself, so too has my life been guided by messengers who have brought God's directions for the path I should follow. My task has been to be open to the messages they bring and to be willing to be led, without worrying where such a willingness will take me—even when it takes me along a path I would not necessarily have chosen on my own. To follow this path is to trust that God is the current in the stream of my life, the force that leads me gently on.

To have that level of trust is more difficult than entering the cold water of a mountain stream; to learn to float more difficult than learning to swim; to surrender far more challenging than trying to struggle; to trust in God's goodness and constant presence far more difficult than assuming I know what is best. But Buddha and Thoreau remind me that to be willing to float, to drift confidently with the current of life, is the only way to the peace and harmony of God.

Easter Sunday

April 2020
Pendle Hill Pamphlet 469

Today is easter sunday in the Christian world of the West—the culmination of the forty days of Lent and the events of Holy Week. Having been raised as a Catholic, I observed all the traditions associated with those events while I was growing up. My family gave up meat during Lent and went to church more frequently. I recall following the Stations of the Cross—tablets depicting Jesus's last week, mounted on the wall in our church—and even watching priests wash one another's feet on Thursday night. However, Easter itself never had much significance for me.

As a teenager, Good Friday was the day that meant the most to me. I would diligently observe the tradition of maintaining silence from noon to 3 p.m., the time Jesus was on the cross, even going off by myself to avoid the temptation to speak to other people. Strangely enough, it's a practice I've continued most of my life, even this week, although if you asked me why I'd have a hard time coming up with an explanation.

As an adult, it is Saturday that has held my attention. Saturday is like an empty space between two events: one has ended, but the other has not yet begun. As I wrote in the essay "Holy Saturday Meditation," it is a day when faith is tested. For me, the faith that is tested is not about who Jesus was, but whether his message is one I believe in and intend to follow, with no other incentive than the meaning of his words and the example of his life.

George Fox encouraged us to turn to the Inward Light to find direction for our lives. He believed that turning to the Inward Light would enable us to see our shortcomings and give us the clarity and strength to change—to strive to overcome worldly temptations and live in harmony with the will of God. Jesus says little about such introspection, as far as I can tell. But many of his comments suggest he believed if we turned inward, we would find that the primary shortcoming we need to overcome is self-centeredness—the constant preoccupation with our own concerns, interests, desires, fears, feelings, and longings. In his sayings, Jesus offers many examples of a solution to that shortcoming—a solution that is on the one hand profoundly simple, and on the other, extremely difficult to put into practice.

In the Gospel of John, Jesus says, "Greater love hath no man than this, that a man lay down his life for his friends." (John 15:13) I have never understood the phrase "lay down his life" to mean to die. I believe the phrase means to be willing to set aside the activities of your own life for a while to help another advance along their journey—to be willing to put another's needs ahead of your own. As in so much of Jesus's teaching, the key word for me is "love." In the same gospel, he says, "A new commandment I give unto you, that ye love one another; as I have loved you, that ye also love one another." (John 13:34) And he says, "For I have given you an example, that ye should do as I have done to you." (John 13:15) What is the example? Washing each of his disciples' feet. John places this event at the end of the meal; that is, in the same position where the other gospels place the story of bread and wine. In doing so, John makes it clear that he believes this—this example of serving the needs of others—is Jesus's primary message, the real meaning of the word love.

When I look at the news these days, the stories that capture my attention are the ones about people helping others during this time of crisis early in the pandemic. I read of medical professionals giving up their regular practice to help people who have the virus; of organizations bringing food to those medical workers in appreciation of their service. I read of people raising money for others who have become unemployed, of people making travel arrangements for students who have been told to return home, and of a man bringing Easter baskets to all the residents of a retirement community near his home. I read of an abundance of acts of kindness and generosity, both large and small.

In my own life, several younger friends have offered to drive me to the one essential doctor's visit I have to do in person. Others call to check up on me, and I find myself checking up on others more frequently and expressing gratitude more regularly to people I usually ignore, like the workers restocking the shelves at

Whole Foods or the lady who diligently cleans the common areas of my apartment building each day. There seems to be a shared understanding that we are all in this together and that we will only come out of it successfully if we are willing to subordinate some of our personal interests to the common good.

The idea that we are all in this together does not just apply to the pandemic; it applies to life on earth itself. And so, I wonder if the current situation will finally enable us to realize that and to understand, both as individuals and as nations, the wisdom of continuing this approach to life together that the current situation has brought forth in so many inspiring ways. Then Easter this year might truly be a resurrection—a resurrection of the spirit of Jesus, and a reminder of the path he encouraged us to follow.

Time and the River

April 2020
Pendle Hill Pamphlet 469

Like many of my friends, I have lost all sense of time. One day seems so much like the one before that I am frequently unsure what day of the week it is. This has led me to think about the angel's words in the book of Revelation that "there should be time no longer." (Revelation 10:6) It feels like that moment has arrived.

Usually, time seems to be individual segments strung together, like beads on a string; events distinguish one day from another and create their separate identity. But time is no longer like that. Now it is a continuous flow, unbroken, undifferentiated, somewhat like living in an endless present, which, a friend reminds me, is what many spiritual philosophies say we should strive to do.

This sense of a continuous unbroken flow reminds me of the image of a stream I wrote about earlier. Right now, it seems more like a river than a stream and that I am traveling in a canoe, moving quietly on the water, rather than floating on my back. The river moves continuously; it has its ebbs and flows, just as in my life there are periods of night and day, but those no longer seem to cut up time into segments any more than the ebbs and flows disturb the unbroken movement of the water.

The things I pass along the river's edge quickly fade from view; some are distinctive enough to remain in memory, while others fade away as soon as I've passed. Even the ones that stand out don't seem to be worth making an effort to remember because I know new and wonderful vistas lie ahead, and it is more enjoyable to look forward to those than to dwell on what's gone by and will never be seen again.

In some places, the river is narrow and the current swift; in others, like now, the river is wide and the current so slow as to be almost imperceptible. In those moments, it's best to relax and be content just to drift, taking the time to observe the world around me with more awareness than I usually do when my sense of passing time makes me rush by. Then I see, as I do now, pink blossoms on cherry trees and purple and red azaleas coming into bloom. I see white blossoms on dogwood trees and wide beds of golden yellow tulips at their base. I notice the sounds of the birds and hear them more distinctly in this moment when the world is more calm and still than usual.

This sense of traveling down a river as an analogy for my life makes me think about the river eventually coming to the ocean and my life eventually coming to its end. I can imagine coming around the last bend in the river after a long and sometimes arduous, sometimes peaceful journey, and suddenly seeing the broad limitless expanse of the ocean before me, sunlight sparkling off the waves. Its breathtaking beauty and vast scale would fill me with awe and joy. Truly it would be like coming into an ocean of boundless love, and I would quite comfortably paddle out into it, willing to be absorbed into its fullness. This image gives me a new perspective on the end of life, not as an end, but as an opening into the expansiveness of something new and wonderful.

The sentence that follows the one about time in the book of Revelation says that then, "the mystery of God should be finished." (Revelation 10:7) I'm not sure what that means. But this new sense of time and the analogy of the river gives me a clearer sense of what that mystery means to me. In my earlier reflection, I said that God is the current of my life, and that's how this continuous unbroken flow of time and the river makes me feel. Just as the current, coming from an unseen source, is the energy that keeps the river flowing, so God is the energy that keeps my life flowing—not just flowing, but also directing its course. I may never know the source of that energy any more than the source of the river's current—that may always remain a mystery—but that doesn't concern me. I can feel the reality of its power and its presence, and that is enough.

Sitting with Jesus

April 2020
Pendle Hill Pamphlet 469

S OME YEARS AGO, I read about a form of prayer in which you envision Jesus present with you and have a conversation with him as you would with a close friend. I've tried that periodically and found it to be an approach that works for me. However, as I thought about this today, I realized that I always envision Jesus sitting opposite me on the other side of the room, which is most likely where a friend would sit. But it felt as if I was intentionally keeping him at a distance, and I thought I should invite him to come over and sit beside me. To do that I needed to move a chair, and that made me wonder whether I should put it to my left or to my right. Where would Jesus like to sit? Where would I like Jesus to sit?

It may seem somewhat silly to worry about where an imaginary Jesus would sit. However, the question turned out to be quite difficult to answer and raised the issue of the difference between my relationship to Jesus and my relationship to God.

To invite Jesus to sit on my right meant that if I reached out to take his hand, or he reached out for mine, he would be holding my right hand—my dominant hand, my hand of control and power—in his left. That implies he'd be leading, and I'd be following. If he sat on the left, I'd have his right hand in my left and that would imply that I was leading and he, while not exactly following, would at least be playing a supportive role. Neither felt comfortable. Although I think of myself as a follower of Jesus, I realized I hadn't been willing to give over the lead to him completely; I was holding something back. On the other hand, sitting him on my left was even more uncomfortable; I knew that if I had to lead, I had no idea where to go or how to get there.

Throughout the gospels Jesus invites many people to follow him. Most of them do, without the slightest hesitation. Of course, it's not literally possible for me to do that, so I've wondered what I mean when I say I'm a follower of Jesus. Initially I felt I meant I was trying to follow his teachings. That led me to write my book *Living in the Kingdom of God* to try to understand what I thought Jesus's teachings really were. What I discovered was that his teachings are primarily about how a person living a spiritually centered life—a person living in what he calls the Kingdom of God—behaves. "Love your enemies, do good to those who hate you" is about behavior—about being nonjudgmental, and being willing to help others regardless of who they are. "Give to whoever asks" is about behavior—being generous. Even Jesus's well-known parables are about people behaving quite differently than what we would normally expect, as examples of people living in the Kingdom of God.

Jesus gives relatively little practical advice about what to do. On the other hand, I feel that throughout my life God has constantly given me guidance about what to do by sending messages via events or people who don't even know they are God's messengers. God has been leading me and I know that will continue to be the case; that's not the issue. The issue is whether I am prepared to surrender control over my life and follow where I am led, and whether I will then behave as a person living in the Kingdom of God should behave. For that I need help and guidance. So, in the end I decide to ask Jesus to sit on my right because I know the bigger challenge is not what to do—God will take care of that—but how to be, and for that I need to follow Jesus's lead. "Follow my way," he will say; "be guided by love, treat everyone with equal respect, be kind and generous, help others as much as you can, and trust God to take care of the rest."

Finding the Way to Walk

April 2021
Friends Journal

Often, I find it helpful to print out a spiritual sentence or phrase and post it somewhere on the wall where I can easily, and casually, see it. This helps to remind me of the message the phrase conveys, but I also find that letting my eyes roll over the words, letting them float around in my mind in a non-intellectual manner, enables me to see something new in them that I don't see when reading the words in their full text. That has been true for a portion of Psalm 143 that I posted on the wall last week.

While the ideas in the verse immediately appealed to me, the more I've looked at it the more I've wanted to reverse the order of the second and fourth phrases. Somehow when I do that, it has much more significance for me. But I worry that by imposing my own conception I may be missing something important in the way the author worded it. My version is this:

> *Cause me to hear thy loving-kindness in the morning;*
> *for I lift up my soul unto thee:*
> *cause me to know the way wherein I should walk;*
> *for in thee do I trust.*

I'll have to confess I don't think much about my soul; the concept of a soul doesn't seem to be part of Quaker spiritual beliefs. So, when I come to that line, the phrase that comes to me that seems to convey the same idea is "open my heart to thee." During this time of self-isolation, the spiritual practice I've been trying to improve is that of meditation. I've tried it before, but I've never been able to sustain it—either for a long enough time in an individual sitting or over time. However, rather than trying to empty my mind of all thoughts as I've done before, I have taken a different approach. Using the words of the psalm, I have been trying to hear God's loving-kindness by opening my heart to God and trying to feel God's presence—feel it within me and also feel that I am being held in God's loving embrace.

God's loving-kindness is always present, of course. The difficulty is getting rid of all the distractions in my mind that prevent me from actually feeling it, from allowing it to permeate my being and transform my life. But consciously trying to open my heart to that presence each morning has enabled me to meditate longer and with a more positive attitude about what I'm doing.

The fact that I trust God leads me on the right path is why I feel more comfortable with that phrase being last. But the word that grabs my attention most is "way." "Way" can have several different meanings. It can mean path or route—which is how I take it in this context—or it can mean *how* to do something, a form of behavior. I've spent a good deal of my life looking for a spiritual path to follow that will lead me into the greater harmony of God. I've at least discovered that I don't want something as definitively defined as a paved sidewalk with clear directional signs. What I want is something more like a dirt path meandering through the woods with occasional side trails to lead me down paths I haven't explored before that open up new experiences and unexpected discoveries. Quakerism is as close as I've come to that, but even its loose structure is often a bit more than I want.

However, as I've been contemplating this verse, it is the second meaning of "way" that has intrigued me. Maybe it's not as important which path you walk, as the *way* (the manner) in which you walk it. After all, there is no real destination, just a journey to be lived, and—who knows—perhaps to walk that journey with love, trust, and an open heart is itself the path, the way, to God.

Cherry Blossoms

May 2020

EACH DAY around noon, I venture outside and take a two-to-three-mile walk. It provides a break in the routine of my day and a break from the monotony of being inside for extended periods of time. I live adjacent to the Benjamin Franklin Parkway, so my walk takes me along Pennsylvania Avenue for several blocks until I come to the place where the freight train line that runs along the edge of the Schuylkill River in Center City emerges from its tunnel. Remarkably enough, there are freight trains still running. For a short distance along the railroad line, there is an area so wild and overgrown that it seems like part of a forest. Small bushes surround tall trees; fallen trees lie where they fell, all sorts of white and yellow and blue flowers cover the ground in the shade and in the sunlight that finds its way through the branches of the trees.

There are two paths through this mini-forest, and to take either would be to feel totally out of the city were it not for the drone of cars and motorcycles on nearby Kelly Drive and the occasional clank of a freight train. The upper path is longer and more frequently used, so I usually take the lower, which is shorter but so enclosed by bushes on both sides that it truly feels like another world. I also like this path because it comes out onto a wide lawn of grass at the edge of which is a bench where I usually stop and rest briefly on my walk.

On this day, about a week ago, it was very windy. I like the wind. I like feeling the air that is always present but invisible to sight or touch. And so, I was quite content. As I approached the bench, I noticed that the wind was blowing the petals of the last of the blossoms off the cherry trees that mark the edge between the forest and the lawn. When I got closer, I saw that the ground around the bench was covered with a remarkably even distribution of the white petals, almost like newly fallen snow. As I wandered back under the large cherry tree, I saw that the entire area beneath it and an adjacent one was totally covered with petals that seemed much more pink than white in the shade but again looked like freshly fallen snow. It was extraordinarily beautiful, and I think it would be accurate to say that "my heart did leap for joy."

When I sat on the bench, the wind continued to blow petals in my direction. They floated gently in the air then settled on the ground before me. It felt like I was sitting in a snow flurry without the cold. The windy day had kept other people away, and so I sat there alone, looking out at the beauty of the scene before me—the wide green lawn, the trees, the blue sky with white clouds floating by—feeling quite peaceful and serene. The wind blew some petals onto my pants and shirt, and I imagined that if I sat there long enough I might become as covered as the ground and merge so totally into this natural environment that I would be virtually invisible to passersby. It was a very pleasant thought.

Recently I'd been watching a video of Louis Armstrong singing the song, *What a Wonderful World*, as an antidote to the world we're living in right now. As I sat there, I could not help but think of the song and some of its lyrics. "I see skies of blue, and clouds of white, the bright blessed day, the dark sacred night." But as I thought of this song, a wave of sadness suddenly washed over me. The world is such a wonderful place, and we are so blessed to be able to be alive on earth; why is there so much hate? Why can't we get along? Why does it take a crisis like the present one to bring out the goodness in people? Why can't we be this way all the time?

Like many others, I am wondering what we will learn from all this. We will go forward to something new and better, or back to the old normal? I know I can't do much about what nations might learn or even what our country as a whole might learn. But the popular phrase—*be the change you want to see in the world* (often mistakenly attributed to Gandhi)—reminds me that it's more important for me to take care of my own little corner of the world.

So, the real question is, what will I learn from this, and how will it change my life? How am I going to go forward to something better rather than back to my old normal? One thing I know for sure, I miss the people I love. I will take them less for granted in the future and express my love for them more frequently—and with abundant physical affection! As for the rest, I'm only beginning to get a sense of some answers, but at least I'm asking a good question.

Trust and Serve

May 2020

Opposite the chair where I sit for my Sunday morning solitary meeting for worship are two bookcases filled with spiritual books. The one on the right consists almost entirely of books about Jesus, indicating the dominance of his teachings in my spiritual life. The one on the left contains a highly diverse collection of books showing my interest in comparative religion and things spiritual. Each speaks to me in a different way. Today it is the books about Jesus that attract my attention. When I look at them, I feel more confused than knowledgeable and wonder how I would summarize his message based on all that I have read.

Jesus himself gives a simple answer to that question. When asked by a lawyer (as the man is called in Luke 10:25) what he must do to inherit eternal life, Jesus mentions only two things: love God with all your heart and love your neighbor as yourself. For me, the word "love" is used in relation to so many different things it has lost its meaning. In the context of these statements, it doesn't really tell me much of practical usefulness, and so I search for other words that convey the same spirit but provide what I think is a clearer sense of what Jesus means or at least what his statement means to me.

It's difficult for me to figure out how to apply the human concepts of love to my idea of God. For me, God is something like an energy field that permeates all creation and encompasses all creation as well. It is an energy field with a special kind of intelligence that gives order to the universe and also influences our individual lives. While it may sound strange to say this, I've always found the concept of The Force in the *Star Wars* movies to be a good approximation.

When I think of an alternative word for love in this context, the one that comes immediately to mind is "trust." To trust first of all that God exists, and then to trust that God is a constant presence in my life that brings only good. To me, that is the "leap of faith," and once I accept that, all else follows as a natural consequence.

To trust in God's presence and goodness is to trust that all the events and experiences of my life are purposeful and meaningful and intended to help me along my spiritual journey. As I said in another reflection, it means to trust that I am being led, to be willing to float in the stream of my life, and confidently accept where the current takes me. It also means to trust that the people who come into my life are messengers sent from God to help me along my spiritual way. No matter what they bring or ask, whether easy or hard, whether they seem friendly or not, all are God's messengers and to be treated with equal respect and loving-kindness.

It is also somewhat difficult for me to understand Jesus's use of the word love with respect to my neighbor.

The word that seems to fit his teachings best is "serve." This is well illustrated in the gospel of John when he says, "Love one another as I have loved you." (John 13:34) and also says, "I have given you an example." (John 13:15) The example is the washing of feet; that is, serving the needs of others. I can modify the word serve in many ways that incorporate the qualities of love—serve with compassion, serve with humility, serve without expecting anything in return, serve anyone in need, serve without worrying about the results or the consequences for yourself. In fact, all these qualities are aspects of love mentioned somewhere in his teachings.

In Wagner's opera, *Parsifal*, the character Kundry has a prominent role in the second act. She is under the spell of an evil master who has charged her to seduce Parsifal so that he will lose the purity he must have to complete his task. She tries very hard and sings a lot! By rejecting her advances, Parsifal essentially frees her from the spell. In the final act, she speaks only one word: Serve. It is the essence of the opera and, I believe, an essential characteristic of Jesus's life and teachings, condensed into a single word.

Of all the thousands of words I've read on the thousands of pages in those couple of hundred books, these two—trust and serve—stand out for me as the ones that best exemplify what it means to lead a spiritual life. They are easy to say but very hard to put into practice. However, many people have been able to do so, which challenges me to continue to strive to do the same.

Alone with God

June 2020

When I sat down for my solitary meeting for worship on Sunday, my mind and heart were on the marches and protests that had occurred in Philadelphia the past Saturday in relation to the killing of George Floyd. It seemed inappropriate to think of anything else, but that's not where I was led.

L<small>AST WEEK</small> during my solitary meeting for worship, my eyes were drawn to the bookcase on the right opposite where I sit, so it is not surprising that this week my attention was drawn to the one on the left. In contrast to the first, which contains books about only one spiritual tradition, the bookcase on the left contains books about so many different spiritual paths it is almost impossible for me to describe what's there. Everything from Buddhism, Islam, and Quakers to *A Course in Miracles*, Gurdjieff, Edgar Cayce, Native American wisdom, Swedenborg—well, you name it, and I probably have at least one book about it.

There is no doubt that I've gained a lot from reading all of them; they have enriched my spiritual knowledge and reinforced many of the ideas I've obtained from the books in the other bookcase. At the same time, they've created a lot of confusion in my mind and for my spiritual journey. When I became a Quaker, I spent about the first ten years trying to learn about the history, spiritual beliefs, and practices of Quakers. That was an inspiring experience and made me feel I'd made the right decision in becoming a member. However, in recent years I have been drawn to the wide variety of other ideas represented by my second bookcase. I liken my approach to trying to get to the top of a high hill or small mountain. I started out on one path and got reasonably far along. But then I decided to explore another path. I went a short way along it, enough to get a feel for it, then tried another and another and another. Now I'm still only partway up the mountain and unsure which path to take and feeling confused and somewhat lost. It feels as if I'm afraid to commit myself to one because I wonder if there might be a better one around the corner or that by picking one I'll pick the wrong one: too many paths, too many choices.

As I was staring at these books today, I realized that the founders of most of these spiritual traditions followed a similar path. Buddha sat under a tree in the forest for forty-nine days, or so the story goes. Jesus went into the desert for forty days; even Muhammad (PBUH) spent many nights week after week in his cave in the hills before anything happened. Native Americans talk about going into the woods on a vision quest. George Fox describes himself wandering alone in the fields at night for what seems like years before he had a transforming opening. Each of them went off alone into a natural environment away from the world of other people. Why did they do this, and what did they do while they were there?

Neale Donald Walsch tells a lovely story that helps explain the "why." A father noticed his young son went off by himself into the woods every day. When he asked his son why he did that, the reply was, "To be closer to God." But, the father said, God is everywhere; God is no different in the woods than here. "Yes, I know that," said the son. "But in the woods *I* am different."

One of the copies I have of the *Tao Te Ching* translates a line as, "Let nature renew what men undo." Clearly, for the young son and for these others, getting away from the man-made world was an important way to get in touch with the essence and wonder of creation and its creator. Anyone who has spent time in a natural setting is aware of the different quality of peace and calm that comes from that experience. That most certainly has been true for me. In such environments, I feel more open and more connected to the divine reality behind creation. The line between myself and the natural world seems to vanish; there is no self, no other, but instead a feeling of complete unity. I am simply one small part of this vast universe and merge into it as gently as a drop of rain falls into the ocean. I believe that's how Buddha, Jesus, Muhammad, Fox, and others felt as well. Did they expect to find God there more than anyplace else? No. As T.E. Lawrence put it, in that "solitude they heard more clearly the living word they brought with them."

As to what they did while there, I cannot say for sure. However, their teachings suggest that they turned inward to connect with that living word they brought with them. While they may not have used these words, they were, it seems to me, all doing what Fox advised early Friends to do: *Turn to the Light within, and it will tell you all you need to know.*

For early Quakers, the idea of turning to the Light within seems to have been both a primary belief and a primary practice. Indeed, it almost seems that it was the only thing early Friends believed in. They were certainly not concerned with codifying a set of rules, ideas, or "testimonies" to follow. Direct experience of what they called the Inward Light seems to have taken precedence even over the Bible. Yet turning to what Friends today call the Inner Light has not been a feature of my own spiritual practice, nor was it for most of the members of several groups of Quakers in different meetings I asked about this. Rather than turning to the Inner Light as a central practice, there seems to be a reliance on other people's experiences that have been organized into a list of testimonies and a book of guidelines without having had the actual experiences ourselves. We know what these others said, but as Fox challenged us, "what canst thou say" of your own direct experience.

Much to my surprise, I have found that sitting silently in my apartment these past weeks has provided the same sense of peace and calm as being in nature, the same feeling of being alone but intimately in touch with God, and more spiritual inspiration (the source of these reflections) than I've found in many months of sitting in a meeting room filled with people. Has this been turning to the Inner Light? I'm not sure, but it seems like a practice worth continuing.

There is a Crack in Everything

June 2020
Pendle Hill Pamphlet 469

TODAY, I DECIDED to hold my solitary meeting for worship on the roof deck of my apartment building. No one was there, so I was able to sit quietly, undisturbed. When I was seated, my eyes were level with the top of the parapet wall that surrounds the deck. Facing west, all I could see was the roof of the Art Museum and, beyond, a thin line of trees in Fairmount Park. Above all that, the vast, open, cloudless blue sky.

My hour passed quickly, my mind coming back now and again to the Black Lives Matter march on the Parkway yesterday protesting the police killing of George Floyd, wondering what the future holds. Just as the alarm on my phone sounded the end of my meeting for worship, a small blue and gray bird landed on top of the parapet. I rarely see birds up here on the fourteenth floor, so it was a bit of a surprise. Usually, when birds are chirping, singing, or speaking—whichever is the right word—I think they have only one sound. But this bird had many, so many that it seemed it was speaking an entire sentence in bird language. Then I realized that this bird must have been designated to close meeting for worship and was saying, "Good morning, John. Peace be with you today." With that, having delivered its message, it flew away.

The bird reminded me of my favorite Leonard Cohen poem and song. It begins with the words, "The birds they sang / At the break of day / Start again / I heard them say." I hear birds singing each morning when I wake up. The sound is a reminder that no matter how well or poorly I lived my spiritual life yesterday, today is a new day, a new beginning, a new opportunity for me to do a little better and inch closer to the person God calls me to be.

Much as I like this line, it is the one that follows that is why I like this poem, "Anthem," so much. "There is a crack, a crack in everything / That's how the light gets in." I doubt if Cohen capitalized "light" when he wrote this poem, but I have no doubt that is what he meant. What is distinctive about the phrase is that a crack is usually considered an imperfection, a defect, a reason for getting rid of the cup or plate or whatever has the crack in it. But Cohen makes it the symbol of something sublimely positive.

I have come to believe that at the moment of our conception, much like the Native American craftspeople and oriental rug makers who deliberately put a flaw in everything to show that only God is perfect, God also puts in each of us something that we, from our human perspective, would call an imperfection or a difficulty. But like the unique skills, talents, and interests God gives us to help us on our spiritual journey, this imperfection or difficulty is also a gift, and all gifts from God are inherently good. In this case, the gift is intended to challenge each of us to love that aspect of ourselves we might most like to be rid of, and through that, learn to love others fully for who they are, even with their own imperfections. It reminds me of a Tibetan Buddhist prayer: "Grant that I may be given appropriate difficulties and sufferings on this journey so that my heart may be truly awakened, and my practice of universal compassion may be truly fulfilled."

For me, I felt the imperfection God had given me was being gay. For the first forty years of my life, I was ashamed of this and worked hard to hide it from others. If a genie in a bottle had come along and offered me one wish, my wish would have been to be "normal," as I would have put it. But there was also something else I kept hidden: I had a deep longing for a spiritual life and for a spiritual community that would accept me as I was. When I came out to my friends, family, and colleagues—when I embraced my imperfection—the Light came through the crack, and my spiritual longing burst forth at the same time. In what I can only describe as an act of God, both came together for the first time when I attended my first Quaker meeting. Since then, both have grown, hand in hand it seems, leading me to a fuller and happier life.

Many people have something they would call an imperfection or a difficulty in life that they would prefer not to have or not to have experienced. And many may believe like I once did, that if that aspect of themselves could be changed, their lives would be much happier. My experience is that the opposite is true: Our imperfection, our difficulty, our crack, is our individual path to wholeness if we are prepared to embrace and follow it—and the path to both the ability to love others in the fullness of who they are, and to unity with God.

Tree Energy

June 2020

For the past two Sundays, my solitary meetings for worship have been anything but peaceful. My mind has been like a corral full of wild horses unwilling to be tamed. It is a reflection, at least in part, I think, of the chaos and confusion that exists in the world around me. I try to calm my mind each morning with a routine of walking, meditation, prayer, and a simple form of Tai Chi, all performed on the roof deck of my apartment building. There are usually no other people there, so I can carry out my activities in the quiet early morning sunlight undisturbed.

The Tai Chi exercise I do is modeled after a form created by Justin Stone. I call it Tree Energy Tai Chi because it is intended to be undertaken with a tree as a partner as a way of reminding myself of the spiritual lessons a tree has to offer. These days, rather than take the time to search out a tree in the park, I focus on a stand of pine trees on the opposite side of the Parkway that I can see from my roof deck, and on one particular tree on the edge that is slightly taller than the others. Each movement of the exercise has a spiritual meaning. The first reminds me that the tree is firmly rooted in the ground; its roots are deep, and its trunk is solid and strong, capable of withstanding all kinds of conditions. This reminds me that my spiritual life must be rooted too, well-grounded in my convictions and practices with confidence in God's presence. The second movement reminds me that the branches of the tree are flexible and can adjust to changing circumstances—wind and rain and snow, different seasons, and temperatures. If the tree was only as stiff as the trunk, it might easily break in a strong wind; if it were only as flexible as the branches that same wind would blow it over. This combination of strength and flexibility, this ability of the tree to accept and adjust to circumstances without losing its integrity, serves as a model and a goal for my spiritual life.

The other movements represent exchanges of energy and love between the tree and me. We each give and we each receive, just as in reality we mutually exchange oxygen and carbon dioxide. The last two movements are the most important. The first requires me to bend my right leg and balance on my left foot while holding my arms folded horizontally in front of my face so that my hands block my view of the tree and everything else. It reminds me that for both me and the tree, the future is uncertain and unknown. The last movement maintains the same position but lifts my arms upward until they and my body form the letter "Y." This symbolizes that no matter what the future brings, I, like the tree, stand ready to receive it with the strength of my faith in God's goodness, and my willingness to accept all that comes to me as a gift. It is a very powerful posture—

and challenging belief—that I hold for sixty seconds before I bow to the tree and finish.

It has somewhat surprised me that, confined as I mostly am to the inside of my apartment, these reflections have been so inspired by thoughts about nature: streams to float in, rivers to float on, hills to climb, birds that sing, and now trees that serve as spiritual teachers. Perhaps the general absence of those things has made them more precious, more a source of spiritual inspiration than usual. And there is even one more: wind.

When I sit, usually shirtless, on the roof deck in meditation after completing my Tai Chi, I feel the wind that comes to me there fourteen floors above the street. It comes as a soft and gentle breeze as if the hands of God were caressing my body with the same soft and gentle touch a mother would use washing a baby's body. It is a final reminder of God's constant presence and loving-kindness that I try to carry with me throughout the day.

Christ in the Midst

June 2020

A WONDERFUL FEATURE OF Zoom technology is that you can attend a meeting for worship almost anywhere. Today I spent part of my time in a Conservative Friends meeting for worship from Cleveland, Ohio, at the invitation of a Conservative Friend I met several years ago. The rest of my time I spent in my usual solitary meeting. The host of the Conservative Friends meeting posted an image on the screen of the painting, "The Presence in the Midst" by James Doyle Penrose. I found this a welcome change from the usual focus on the faces of participants.

The painting is based on the gospel of Matthew, 18:20: "For where two or three are gathered together in my name, there I am in the midst of them." Penrose's interpretation of the phrase is clearly influenced by George Fox's statement, "Christ has come to teach his people." This is indicated by the hovering transparent figure of Jesus superimposed over a seventeenth or early eighteenth-century meeting for worship in what is thought to be Jordans Meeting House in England. Women in bonnets and plain dress and men in dark suits and hats sit with heads bowed in silent, expectant worship. The image, and my interpretation of the gospel phrase, reminded me of the difference between meeting for worship alone and with others.

All my life, I have been aware that I feel very different when I am in the presence of another person. I feel more alert, more alive, more energized whether I'm with just one person or many. And it doesn't seem to matter whether we are in the same room or separate ones or whether we are doing something together or not. The mere presence of another person nearby is enough to change my attitude and the way I feel. I have a theory of why this is so.

I believe that all living things are sending out vibrations of energy. When I am with someone else, the vibrations of energy we are each sending out interact with one another to enhance and magnify our own individual energies and create a new and third field of energy that both combines our individual energies and encompasses them as well. It is like saying there is me, and there is you, but then there is also "us," which is a third entity in its own right that results from the merger of the two of us and in some strange way is greater than the sum of its individual parts.

There is some basis in scientific fact for this theory. Scientists tell us that at the atomic level, everything is in motion; everything is vibrating and sending off waves of energy whether we detect it or not. This is true of even what we might call "dead" matter—rocks and other inanimate objects. The only difference is that living creatures, and human beings especially, send off waves of energy at higher frequency levels. Some scientists suggest that there must be an intelligent force that sets these atomic movements in motion. For me, that force is what I mean when I use the word God.

When I apply these ideas to meeting for worship, it is the words "come together *in my name*" that have special significance. I don't take those words as literally referring to Jesus, as Penrose did. To me, they mean coming together with the specific *intent* to try to connect with "that of God" within, with the Inner Light or what some call the "Christ consciousness" that Jesus personified so fully and that is potential in all of us. And in the best of moments, that effort brings forth an encompassing field of energy—a presence—that unites each of us with one another and with the Divine energy of creation itself.

When I am in meeting for worship with others—even just two or three—the potential for this sense of a larger field of energy is greater than when I am alone. I believe that this sense of connection to something larger enables me or another to tap into the presence within and bring forth a message that may provide one or more of us present with inspiration for our spiritual journey. This potential, and the feeling that I am vibrating in unity with the oneness of all creation that seems only possible in the actual physical presence of others, is what I miss in the current situation and long to recapture.

Siddhartha

July 2020
Pendle Hill Pamphlet 469

During the past weeks, I've been rereading books I read many decades ago and finding that they often provide a source of inspiration for my solitary meetings for worship. This week the book was *Siddhartha* by Hermann Hesse. I discovered Hesse in my twenties and read nearly all his novels, including *Siddhartha*, which I've read several more times in the intervening years.

The main character has the same first name as the man who becomes the Buddha and his early life experiences are so similar to those of Buddha that at first it seems that is who the novel is about. But this is not the case. Siddhartha is a different person who eventually meets the enlightened Buddha and listens to his teachings. Although he is impressed by Buddha and concludes his teachings are worthy of profound respect, he doesn't become a follower.

It is his reason for continuing on his own that captures my attention now. Basically, he says that to accept anyone else's beliefs, no matter how true they may seem, is to accept what they have found just as you would accept a set of man-made laws or rules to follow without participating in their creation. They are not true to your own experience but are something you adopt and put on like a pre-made coat that fits you well. Even Buddha seems to share this concern to some degree; he tells his followers that if they really want to find enlightenment, they should sit under a tree and meditate. That is, he says, follow my example; test my conclusions on your own. A contemporary saying—"If you meet the Buddha on the road, kill him"—points to the necessity of finding enlightenment on your own, not by adopting someone else's results.

So Siddhartha moves on with his personal search. He has a variety of experiences, eventually becoming an assistant to a ferryman and then the ferryman himself. He never reaches an "aha!" moment of enlightenment, but in the end, he reaches his own form of enlightenment and peace. "What interests me," he says, "is being able to love the world, not scorn it, and not to hate it and hate myself, but to look at it and myself and all beings with love and admiration and reverence."

Many years ago, I heard a statement attributed to George Fox in which he said his task was to bring people to Christ and leave them there. It seems to me that statement is much like Buddha's: *Don't accept what I have found just because I found it and it sounds good to you. You have to find it for yourself; turn inward and see what you discover on your own.* I wonder if Margaret Fell might have been right about us today when she said, upon first hearing Fox preach about Christ: "We are all thieves." Have we simply accepted what early Friends discovered through experience without following their example, because to accept what they found is easier and more comfortable than having the experience ourselves?

When I attended Quaker meeting for the first time, everything seemed to fit perfectly—silent meeting for worship, the testimonies, and other Quaker practices. It was like going into a store and finding that a suit had already been made for me, tailored to my exact measurements even before I arrived. I put it on and have worn it comfortably for many years. It hasn't entirely gone out of style; it still seems to be a reasonable fit and has served me well. But *Siddhartha*, and these past weeks of being alone, have made me wonder about my decision and made me conscious of the fact that I did not choose the material or the color or the style but accepted what someone else had determined and put it on without much hesitation.

Siddhartha and being alone have also made me wonder about the importance of a solitary search as contrasted with the importance of being part of a spiritual community. Being part of a spiritual community seems most relevant once you have accepted a common set of spiritual beliefs. But seeking seems to be a solitary task, one we must each undertake on our own if we want to find something that will truly transform our lives.

I am reminded that in the Hindu tradition, when a man reaches my age he is expected to leave his family, leave his community, give up all possessions, and set out alone on a solitary spiritual journey. There is even a ceremony to mark this moment during which the man burns a copy of the Vedas, the Hindu equivalent of the

Bible, to symbolize that whatever god he will henceforth follow is one he will have to find on his own. So, when this pandemic is over, if you see me wandering aimlessly through the streets of Philadelphia, don't wonder if I'm lost; wonder instead if I have chosen that path and wish me well.

Black Jesus

July 2020

There are four objects on the bookcase next to the desk where I write these reflections that are evidence of my interest in comparative religion. One is a statue of Buddha. Another is a square orange ceramic tile with the word for Allah in Arabic in red letters, and the third, a colorful statue of the Hindu god Hauman—the monkey god—about whom I know very little. The fourth statue is of Jesus and is a somewhat unusual one, at least for me.

The approximately twelve-inch-tall statue portrays Jesus as a Black man with short black hair and a black mustache and goatee. He is standing on what looks like a cloud, with arms extended outward at his sides. His only garment is a blue robe wrapped around his body and head, leaving one arm and most of his dark-skinned chest exposed. Although it is quite simple, whoever designed the statue has been able to convey the sense of dignity, strength, and self-confidence Jesus must have had, and, through his outstretched arms, a sense of his kindness and compassion.

When I found this statue in a vendor's cart at the 30th Street Amtrak Train Station, it had an immediate and powerful impact on me. Today the statue has even more meaning because of the events of the past weeks and the encampment (advocating for housing) created by the Black Lives Matter movement that has taken over the baseball fields along the Benjamin Franklin Parkway opposite my apartment building. There are around 100 or so tents in the encampment, and I can readily imagine my Black Jesus wrapped in his blue blanket emerging from one of them ready to preach his message of love to any assembled homeless followers much like he preached his message to what might have been similar followers in his day.

My fascination with this statue is not because I care about the color of Jesus's skin. I am sure he was not the Northern European white man with long, nicely combed hair and spotlessly clean clothes as he is typically depicted. But I think it is also unlikely that he was Black, and if he was of darker skin, undoubtedly so were the other people in his community, and therefore he would not have stood out as anything unusual. But depicting him as a Black man does have special significance today. It is a reminder that he too was oppressed, and not valued by much of his society. It is also a reminder that he identified more with poor and marginalized people to whom he brought his message than with the well-to-do and well-established. Above all, it expresses to me in a profound way that there is "that of God in everyone" and that everyone can be God's messenger—a belief that is particularly important to me right now as I stare out at the homeless encampment in front of me.

The statue makes me wonder if I would have been attracted to Jesus's message when I was younger if he had been depicted as a Black man in the Catholic Church I attended. Or even whether his teachings would have the same relevance today to the Italian Catholics of South Philadelphia. Or conversely, would his message to love one another, even those who oppress you, have been more powerful coming from someone whose condition provided no good reason to think in those terms and every reason to think otherwise. Would that message, coming from a Black man, have created a different attitude about Black people in general that would have led to a different society than the one that has prevailed so long in this country?

In addition to these thoughts about Jesus, the statue and recent events pose a question about God that I have not considered before. Is my entire conception of God distorted by my perspective as a privileged white man? I grew up with the image of God as an elderly bearded white man on a cloud in the sky, and so it is not surprising that this has influenced my perspective. I began to address the "male" aspect of that many years ago by consciously refusing to refer to God as "he," even if it required me to repeat the word God many times in the same sentence. However, I haven't been willing to alternate "he" with "she" as some often do. My reluctance is because I no longer think of God in anthropomorphic terms. I think of God as a Divine Spirit or as a Divine Energy. For those definitions of God, the correct pronoun is "it," something I've been comfortable with ever since reading a character use that term in the novel *The Color Purple*.

But while I've considered that issue, I have not considered whether white privilege has influenced my perspective. That is a new challenge. I think of God as a positive presence in my life and that all the gifts I have received from God are good and designed to help me on my spiritual journey. It is quite easy for me to think in those terms because I've basically had a very blessed life. I've had my share of struggles and difficulties, but my life has been relatively easy by comparison with many others. I have no doubt that this is partly because I am white, male, well-educated, and have benefited from all the unearned privileges that come with those characteristics. But has that unconsciously influenced my concept of God? Has my thinking of God from my perspective as a white man implicitly made me value white people more than people of color?

Would my conception of God be the same if I was a homeless Black man living across the street in a tent? Or if I was an employed low-wage-earning man living in a run-down and crime-ridden neighborhood of North Philadelphia? Or a Black woman trying to raise two children while living in public housing? What would my conception of God be in those circumstances? Could I believe that everything that had come to me was a gift and a good gift at that? Or would my conception of God remain the same, but my faith be stronger, like those communities in South America who find strength in the fact that Jesus also suffered and yet could still love and forgive those who oppressed him.

I think it is because of the difficulty of holding a positive image of God in such circumstances that I so greatly admire the faith of Black people, whether Christian or Muslim or of any other faith tradition. For many years I worked with the head of the community association in an impoverished and racially segregated neighborhood in North Philadelphia. I was twenty-six years old when I first went there and found myself in a world unlike anything I had previously experienced or could possibly have imagined. Within the five or ten minutes it took me to walk from the trolley stop to this man's house, my entire life changed. I suddenly realized that the picture of the world my parents and teachers had painted was not accurate, and that the comfortable world in which I lived was at the expense of others who had to live in poverty, confined to racially segregated neighborhoods.

When I stood on his doorstep, ready to ring the doorbell, I noticed a bumper sticker pasted on the window beside the door. During the many decades I worked with him, he lived in several different houses in the neighborhood, but in each one, he had this bumper sticker pasted to his front window. It said, "*God is Good All the Time.*" Each time I went to his house, I stood in awe that someone living in the conditions in which he did could believe that. But he did; he most emphatically did. He may not have had many material possessions, but his spiritual possessions were substantial and a source of inspiration to me. He made me more appreciative of the gifts I had received and made me more conscious of the need to share my unearned and perhaps undeserved good fortune with others. Today the statue of Black Jesus beside me is a constant reminder of all that and a continuing source of inspiration and challenge.

Marcus Aurelius

July 2020
Pendle Hill Pamphlet 469

Although I call my meetings for worship "solitary meetings," many friends have come by to join me. George Fox is pretty much always here, as are Buddha and Jesus. Lao Tzu and Henry David Thoreau have dropped in, along with Siddhartha and Leonard Cohen, as well as birds and trees, to name a few. Each one has brought a spark of inspiration that opened a door to something within that brought a new and helpful insight for my spiritual journey.

Today my companion was Marcus Aurelius, an old friend—over 2,200 years old, in fact—who stops by from time to time to whisper words of wisdom in my ear. I imagine him sitting beside me outfitted like a Roman general in a Hollywood movie or TV miniseries even though he's a philosopher at heart. Marcus is a Stoic; he believes in many gods, but his primary one seems to be "Nature" or what he calls "Reason." Nonetheless, he's one of those people of whom it can be said that they are Quakers without really knowing it. In his *Meditations* he says, "The spirit-God gave each of us to lead and guide us, a fragment of himself," which I think comes close enough to "that of God in everyone" to qualify him for honorary membership in the Religious Society of Friends.

When I browse through Marcus's *Meditations*, I am impressed with how remarkably timeless his ideas are and how much he anticipated the spiritual thoughts of many later people, most of whom I suspect were unfamiliar with his work. When he says, "All things are woven together and the common bond is sacred, and scarcely one thing is foreign to another" or "There is one universe out of all, one God through all," his words are almost the same as those attributed to Chief Seattle reminding us that "Man did not weave the web of life; he is merely a strand in it."

As a Stoic, Marcus is essentially a fatalist, but not in a negative or pessimistic sense of that word. He believes in Fate—that each person has a Destiny that is inescapable and unavoidable, and therefore necessary to accept: "Be content with what happens to you: first because it was for you it came to pass, for you it was ordered and to you it was related, a thread of destiny stretching back to the most ancient causes." But he does not encourage us to accept that destiny with a sense of resignation: "Welcome *with affection*," he says, "what is sent by fate." His philosophy anticipates Nietzsche's *amor fati*—love your fate. Welcome it, they both say; embrace it, live it to its fullest as if it was the destiny you would have chosen for yourself out of all the possible destinies God might have offered you.

In a quite remarkable way, Marcus anticipates the current mindfulness movement of living in the present moment. When he says, "Man lives only in the present, in this fleeting instant; all the rest of his life is either past and gone, or not yet revealed," it's hard to know whether it's Marcus speaking or Eckert Tolle or even Thich Nhat Hanh. And despite his own difficulties, Marcus expresses the same attitude that Shakespeare states more eloquently in *Hamlet*, that "There is nothing either good or bad, but thinking makes it so." But Marcus also reminds us that we can change our attitude at any moment and see all as good, for if all things are gifts of the gods, they must be good, and therefore we should accept them in that spirit knowing that "whatever happens, happens rightly." These are challenging ideas and sometimes hard to embrace, but they have a ring of truth about them that is enhanced by the simplicity and directness of his language.

When Marcus departs, I try to put his thoughts into simple phrases that will be easy for me to remember. Two emerge by which I increasingly try to live my life. The first is trust. *Trust without fear* is the concept Marcus leaves me with. Trust in God's goodness and do not fear life or anything in life, including death, which is a part of life. The second is acceptance; *acceptance without complaint* was the way I first put it, but *acceptance with gratitude* is, I think, a better phrase and a better attitude that encourages me to see and accept life's difficulties in a different light, along with its blessings.

As I enter my eighth decade, there are many personal reasons for fear and, as I look at the world around me, there are many grounds for complaint if I want to go down those paths. Trust and acceptance are much harder to come by and wholeheartedly embrace, which I guess is why Marcus returns from time to time to beat those two words into my head and heart. But despite his Stoicism, he always leaves on a positive and challenging note: "What remains except to enjoy life, joining one good thing after another, so as to leave not even the smallest interval unfulfilled?"

Thank you, old friend; come again.

Eid al-Adha

August 2020
Pendle Hill Pamphlet 469

TODAY IS the middle of a four-day period that marks the celebration of Eid al-Adha in Islam. This is the commemoration of Abraham's willingness to sacrifice his son as an indication of his faith in God, or, as Muslims would more likely put it, to surrender his will to the will of God. The commemoration is celebrated by Muslims worldwide, usually through the sacrifice of an animal and the sharing of one-third of its meat with friends and relatives and one-third with the poor. It is also a feature of the Hajj, the annual pilgrimage to Mecca that occurs at this time, during which certain aspects of Abraham's story are reenacted.

The story of this incident in Abraham's life appears in both the Bible and the Qur'an. In both cases, the central issue appears to be the test of Abraham's faith, and therefore both versions implicitly ask the question, what is faith? However, the version in the Qur'an includes elements not found in the biblical version that raise another question central to the issue of faith, which is particularly relevant to me as a Quaker.

In the Qur'an, God, through the angel Gabriel, tells Abraham to sacrifice his son. (The son's name—Abraham has two sons—is not mentioned.) However, in this version, not only does Gabriel appear to Abraham, but so does Satan. Satan tries three times to convince Abraham not to sacrifice his son. Each time the angel Gabriel tells Abraham to "pelt him," that is, throw stones at Satan to drive him away, which Abraham successfully does. This is one of the aspects of the story reenacted during the Hajj.

The fact that God and Satan both appear to Abraham raises a critical question: If you want to make a leap of faith, how do you know for sure it is God speaking to you and not Satan? For Abraham, knowing the difference between God and Satan was not a problem; God was a tangible presence in his life, speaking to him directly and clearly. But for the rest of us, this is not usually true, so we must find other ways to discern when we believe it is God that is calling.

This has been a central question in my life, particularly when it comes to trying to discern what Quakers refer to as "leadings"—a call to undertake a particular activity you believe comes from God. Indeed, I have often wondered if what I think has been God's presence in my life might very well have been Satan's (in whom I don't really believe) and that I have constantly made all the wrong choices. My theory is that we often think we're led to do something that appears to be good—and usually is good—but is a lesser good than the one we are capable of. This false leading is a deliberate distraction to lead us away from a greater good God is calling us to perform. Consequently, trying to discern the difference between a true and false leading based on the character of the outcome is not a reliable test.

As I have struggled with this issue over the years, I have found that certain characteristics help me have greater confidence that it is God who is calling me to take some action. The word "leading" is a good choice because I feel that I am not being *told* what to do; I am being invited to consider the possibility of doing something that is initially often vague or unclear. I may be motivated by a concern, but there is an element of doubt about whether I am being called to respond to it at all and, if so, in what way.

In those situations, the first test for me is *persistence*. If it is a true leading, it doesn't go away. I can ignore it or even reject it, but it will return—perhaps not immediately and perhaps not in the exact same form, but it will return. For me, this is much like the story of Jonah and the whale. Jonah rejects God's request to go to Nineveh and preach and instead hightails it in the opposite direction. But God is persistent, and eventually Jonah has no choice but to relent.

The next test is whether I am being called to do something *outside my normal comfort zone*, something I feel I am *not really qualified* to do. If that is the case, I am naturally reluctant to undertake what is apparently being asked of me. Like Jonah, it's something I'd rather avoid. But at the same time, I have a sense of foreboding about it. I like the word foreboding. I picked it up from an interview with the actor Daniel Day-Lewis, who used it to describe how he felt when trying to decide whether to take a particular movie role. He said he had a sense of foreboding that he wasn't going to be able to avoid it and had best get on with doing it. Foreboding implies hesitancy and reluctance, as well as danger and risk—a venturing into unknown territory with an uncertain outcome yet feeling compelled to go forward anyhow. That's the same sense I have in following a leading; it is more like a *surrender to the inevitable* than a task undertaken eagerly with confidence and joy. If it feels like something that I'm naturally interested in, something I feel capable of doing, and am willing to undertake eagerly, it is likely to be a lesser good and not a true leading. A true leading is almost precisely the opposite, something to approach with "fear and trembling."

Quakers offer another test contained in the phrase "way opens:" If a leading is true, then once you embark on it, resources or assistance will come along to help you. If not, then that is a sign not to proceed further. That has been true for me, but with a significant element added. Once I have decided to surrender to God's will and follow the leading, I am filled with a sense of peace and contentment that comes from the act itself, from giving myself over to the current I've talked about before rather than struggling against it, and feeling the peace and joy that comes from that surrender.

Although all these tests help me to be more confident that my leading is from God, the truth is I can never know for certain, which brings me back to the question of faith. It does not seem to me that Abraham's situation is a test of his faith. He knows it is God who is speaking to him, and God is giving him a clear and direct order. Unless he wishes to reject his entire past relationship with God, he has no choice except to obey. For Abraham, there is no doubt, there is only certainty; to my mind, his issue is obedience, not faith. In the Qur'an, Abraham tells his son that God has told him to kill him. His son has many choices: he can run; he can reject the idea and refuse to cooperate; he can struggle and even resist being bound on the mountain. But in telling his son, Abraham almost appears to be asking for his advice, for his recommendation of what to do. His son has no direct relationship with God telling him what to do, yet he says that if it is God's will, then Abraham should go ahead and do it. He voluntarily agrees to surrender his life, not by virtue of following God's command—and not by following a leading—but simply by virtue of faith in whatever God he believes in. It seems to me that the test of faith is that of the son, not the father. For faith, much like following a leading, is a *voluntary surrender* to what you believe but cannot know for certain is the will of God—a leap into the unknown, a risk undertaken in fear and trembling with no assurance as to the outcome.

Healing Begins

August 2020

Healing begins when we each take responsibility for our part in the pain.

I SPOKE THOSE WORDS in a meeting for worship at Friends General Conference almost twenty-five years ago. The words, and the ones that followed, came from that place where spirit-led messages originate, not from any clear thinking of my own. The meeting for worship was focused on racial healing. There were about fifty or sixty White Quakers present, along with six Black Quakers, five women and one man. What prompted my message was a question I asked myself: What did the six Black people need to hear from us? It came to me that an apology was in order, and that idea opened the door for the spirit to put the words in my mouth. They still seem relevant today—more relevant in fact—and suggest a possible way to begin to move forward. These are the words, as best I remember them, the spirit led me to speak back then:

"Healing begins when we each take responsibility for our part in the pain. I know that the pain of racial discrimination is not part of the past, not just a part of the period of slavery. I know that it has extended into my own lifetime and up to the present moment. I know that my parents, friends, and I have implicitly condoned it. I would like to apologize for myself and my society, White society, and all that we have done to you and your ancestors. I hope you will forgive us. For myself, I pledge that I will strive in my own life to make sure it does not continue."

My message was not directed toward the White people present. I was not saying, here is something I think we need to do. It was explicitly directed to the six Black people who sat in front of me and was intended to come from me personally to them personally and individually. Moreover, I was not then, and I am not now, asking for forgiveness: that seems inappropriate and is simply a way to relieve myself of the burden of guilt. I can only apologize, and if forgiveness is offered or not, that was and still is a decision for them to make. And if it is withheld—withheld until I truly earn it by my present and future actions—then that would be appropriate and just.

I felt strongly then and continue to feel today that the White society I—and most of you who are reading this—are part of, owes a genuine, sincere, and explicit apology to the Black citizens of our community and country. We may think that by passing civil rights legislation, by passing laws to overcome discrimination, by supporting anti-poverty programs, that by doing all those things we have taken responsibility for the past and apologized, but in truth, we have not. We need to say it explicitly and directly to both the Black society as a whole and individual Black people, as I tried to do at FGC.

When I look at the Black Lives Matter movement and ask myself, what can I do, what should we—White society—do, I come back to that phrase: Healing begins when . . . The Black Lives Matter movement has offered us an open invitation and expressed the hope that we will take up that challenge to acknowledge our part in the pain and begin the healing process. As a start we need to apologize; we need to connect with one another and get to know one another as real people; we need to know one another's hopes and dreams, the things we share in common so that we can truly see that we are all part of one human family with the same hopes and dreams for our lives and the lives of our children. An apology may not be enough; there may be a need for reparations or other solutions. But it is an essential place to begin, a place of intimate human connection, and out of that whatever is needed to heal will arise and be valued more because it will be something we determine together. It will be an expression of our love and respect for one another.

It is not likely that this will be effective or have the impact that is needed unless we do this as communities of people seeking reconciliation with one another. What is needed is an extended dialogue and an organized way to conduct it.

Although this is something I'd like to see all Philadelphia undertake, it is a process that Quakers could begin and hope that others might follow. Let us declare a Year of Reconciliation. Let each of our meetings reach out to a religious congregation in the Black community—preferably one that is also geographically and economically different—and ask to be allowed to offer an explicit apology for our own and our society's actions. Then let us begin a sustained yearlong process of listening, getting to know one another as people and seeing what solutions for future change God may inspire us to find together. At the end of a year, we can come together to share results.

I feel it is essential to do this in person, so it may not be possible to begin until the Covid-19 crisis has ended or eased. But we can start now to identify partners and plan how to go about this, even testing out some ideas via Zoom. Alone and separate we will continue to stumble; together we may be able not only to find a way to heal the pain, but also a path toward a world in which all God's children will know only love and respect.

Look for the Good

August 2020

One of the readers of these reflections sent me a music video of a song entitled *Love is Still the Answer*. I found this so inspiring I looked for other videos by the same artist, Jason Mraz. That led me to *Look for the Good*, which I found equally inspiring. Now I play each one several times a week as a source of inspiration. In addition, I printed out the words to the chorus of *Look for the Good* and posted it on a wall where I've started to put up quotes that inspire me. In the time I spent in solitary meeting for worship this morning, it was those words I thought about—almost as if they were a message someone else in meeting with me had just delivered.

Looking for the good in everyone has an obvious connection to the Quaker belief that there is "that of God" in everyone. Much as I believe that and find it helpful, it is sometimes too general and too conceptual to have an impact on how I behave. On the other hand, "look for the good" is simple, direct, tangible, clear, easy to remember, and gives me a proactive orientation to the way I view other people and events.

When I thought about this phrase this morning, I was reminded that most of the time, I consider myself a "glass half empty" type of person. I tend to see the difficulties and problems first. Quite often, that helps me identify things I can do something about, but most of the time it means that I feel weighed down by the burden of these problems. As another song says, I feel I walk around with "my blues on parade." My usual reaction to this feeling has just been to hope the problems and difficulties will go away, hope that things will improve in the future. But valuable as a feeling of hope can be, it can also be an obstacle, as Thich Nhat Hanh points out. When "We cling to our hope in the future, we do not focus our energies and capabilities on the present moment. If you can refrain from hoping you can bring yourself entirely into the present moment and discover the joy that is already here." That certainly is true for me, and so I have decided to abandon all hope and simply look for the good that's in the present around me right now.

That seems like a crazy thing to do when the world seems to be in such a mess. But I'm starting to feel that makes it even more important to look for the good— to recognize and appreciate the good that is there, to believe that some good will come of all that seems to be a mess right now, and to set about trying to find it. While Jason reminds us that it may seem "impossible to find until it's done," he also suggests it's there if we are willing to look for it, and that life—our own life, everyone's life—"would be sweeter if everybody would."

If you are seeking inspiration to help you start looking, join me in watching Jason Mraz's music videos for *Look for the Good* and *Love is Still the Answer*.

Hope

August 2020

LAST WEEK I reflected on how hope could be an obstacle to appreciating and experiencing the joy and wonder of the present moment. This week, while meditating in the morning, I recalled those thoughts and found myself reflecting on the opposite—how hope can be a positive influence and give strength during difficult times. That reflection was influenced by a recent video chat with the young man I visit in prison. He is serving a term of life without parole, but despite that, he has a remarkably positive and optimistic attitude about his life. I sometimes feel he is more positive and optimistic than I am, despite the difference in our circumstances.

His attitude is, in part at least, influenced by his religious beliefs. He is a Muslim and takes his religious practices seriously; he fasts during Ramadan and does his best to pray five times a day within the context of his prison schedule. He believes that where he is right now—where each of us is right now—is precisely where Allah intends him (and us) to be, and therefore all is to the good. He acknowledges that being sent to prison has had a positive impact on his life, transforming him from a drug dealer and convicted criminal into a more thoughtful and responsible man.

While I think I would find a life sentence demoralizing, he is sustained by the hope that appeals may shorten his sentence. Over the fifteen years he has been in prison, he has done a good job of educating himself about the law and has filed many appeals, pointing out irregularities in his trial. Even though so far all of those have been turned down, he has not lost hope.

The appeals process is like climbing a ladder. Each time you go up one rung and get rejected, that allows you to move up to the next higher rung until finally you get near the top where, in some instances, a favorable outcome might be more likely. He's almost at the top right now and waiting for the result. But recently, he said that if his latest appeal is rejected, he will apply to have his sentence commuted based on his positive accomplishments in prison. So there is still room to hope, and I believe this contributes to his ability to maintain such a positive outlook.

At first, his example served to remind me that there are two aspects of hope. Yes, it can be an obstacle to living in the present moment, but it can also be the factor that makes it possible to live positively in the difficult circumstances of the present moment. So, my previous conclusion to abandon all hope seems a little too extreme. But the more I thought about his situation, the more I realized that he embodies a good balance between these two aspects of hope. In the present, he is taking advantage of whatever the prison has to offer in educational courses, focusing on subjects that may be of use to him if he gets out, but often taking things simply for the experience of learning something new. He has written one short book about his relationship with his daughter and is now completing a book of poems. He is very focused on making the most out of the present moment to the fullest extent his circumstances allow. He is not pinning all his "hopes" on a future that may or may not occur. On the other hand, neither is he just sitting back and idly hoping that something good will happen in the future. He's taking whatever action he can to help the future he hopes for appear.

So now I see that both aspects of hope have their worthwhile qualities. The key is to find the balance between pinning your hopes on the future to such a degree that you miss out on the joy and wonder of the present and focusing so much on the present that you neglect to do your part in helping a positive future emerge.

The Certainty of Faith

September 2020
Pendle Hill Pamphlet 469

BEFORE THE PANDEMIC arrived, I used to go to the Chapel of Divine Love a few blocks from my apartment building to meditate each morning. It was always empty except for one nun keeping vigil near the altar, so I could sit in silence undisturbed for as long as I wanted. Even though the chapel has reopened, I'm hesitant to enter, and instead I walk about in the small garden adjacent to it and then sit on a stone wall for a period of meditation. While I was there the other day, a man and a woman approached the door of the adjacent convent where the nuns who support the chapel live in cloistered isolation. Few people ever go to the convent door while I'm there, so just their arrival itself was somewhat of a surprise.

The man was older, perhaps fifty, but I could not tell the age of the woman. She had dark hair and was wearing a black mask that covered most of her face. The man held her by the elbow, guiding her up the few steps to the entrance door. They rang the bell and were admitted immediately, which made me think they had been expected. I had the instantaneous feeling that I was watching the man escort his daughter, wife, sister—someone he cared deeply about—who had come to join the convent. The mere idea sent a tremor through my body that left me standing motionless on the walk, staring at the now empty space in front of the door. The tremor was not one of fear but of awe at what I imagined I was witnessing at that moment—awe for the woman and the commitment she was about to make; awe for the man who had the courage to bring her there and leave her, perhaps never to see her again. It did not matter whether what I imagined was true or not—and I don't know if it was—but at some point in the past, another woman and man had made that journey, and these two were merely a reminder of that. As I sit here this morning, the feeling of awe is still with me four days later.

When I was twenty-three, I visited the Trappist monastery in Spencer, Massachusetts. Those were the days when Trappists observed a strict rule of silence. I went to study the architecture, a beautiful stone complex modeled after monasteries of the Middle Ages in Europe. But what overwhelmed me was the sense of serenity and peace that permeated the entire place. I can still recall sitting in the visitors' side alcove of the chapel listening to monks I could not see intoning Gregorian chant and feeling more at peace and in harmony with God than I had ever felt before. When it came time to leave, I was tempted to tell the friends I'd come with to go along without me; I was going to stay. I didn't. The desire to experience life in the world was too great, but the longing for something I felt there has never left me.

I feel this same longing whenever I see someone who has made such a strong commitment to a spiritual life that they are willing to show it publicly in their dress, their words, or their behavior, whether that be spreading a prayer rug on the sidewalk to pray at the right time or handing out Christian literature on a street corner. This is particularly true of young men because as a man I identify more easily with men. It does not matter what their religious affiliation is. The simple commitment to let their spiritual life be a dominant and visible influence on the rest of their life strikes a chord in my heart that confronts me with the reality that no matter how much I've thought and written about spiritual life, there is a certainty of faith that still eludes me.

Earlier I wrote about the Buddhist concept of "entering the stream" and used the image of floating in the water and allowing the current to carry you where it will as an analogy for letting God be the spiritual current that moves the stream of your life. For myself, I feel I've been knee-deep in the stream for a long time, standing motionless in cold mountain water, hesitant to dive in and turn over and float. I can feel the current pushing against me, I watch the water flow by, I feel the desire to dive in, but something is holding me back; something prevents me from taking the plunge and surrendering my life completely to a larger force outside my own control.

For most of my life, my spiritual goal has been to "be in the world but not of it." That is hard to do, and I have still not achieved it. But I now realize this is not what I have truly wanted; what I want is to be "not of the world, but in it." In the first, no matter how much spiritual integrity you live with, the world is still the dominant context of your life. In the second, spiritual life is the dominant context, and when you allow the world to enter, it is in more limited ways and on more limited terms.

The certainty of faith seems to me to be a solitary act: No one can take the plunge into the stream for you; no one but you can make the leap of faith. But the courage to make that move is undoubtedly enhanced by knowing that there is even just a small group of friends standing in the water with you, encouraging you to take the plunge, and ready to float along with you or standing by to catch you if you leap and fall. That does not require entering a monastery or a convent, but it does seem to require at least a few like-minded individuals equally committed to a similar spiritual life, with whom you are engaged on almost a daily basis, and with whom the primary subject of your interaction is providing the mutual spiritual support that enables your entire life to be grounded in God.

That combination of the certainty of faith—a certainty that comes even in the face of the uncertainty about what can truly be known—and a supportive community is what I felt when I visited the monastery, what I imagined in the man and woman at the convent door, what I think when I see young men visibly displaying their commitment to a spiritual way of life, what I long for and have not yet found.

Holding in the Light 2

September 2020

Last week I was informed that an acquaintance from Chestnut Hill Friends Meeting was in intensive care, sedated, and on a ventilator. Whether this was from Covid-19 or another reason, I do not know. I refer to him as an acquaintance rather than a friend not to diminish my feeling for him, but because I only knew him in that limited way you know people in your Quaker meeting with whom you have no other social or personal connection. My closest contact with him came once a year when I organized the meeting's annual art show. He was always eager to display and discuss his artwork and occasionally helped organize and hang the show. I also know he liked dancing, although I never saw him dance. My impression was that he had a difficult life and struggled with both financial and health issues. I may be wrong, but that's the impression I had, and it's that impression, combined with his present circumstances, that weighed heavily on my heart this morning as I sat in my usual solitary meeting for worship.

Some Friends have organized sessions to hold him in the Light, so that is what I am trying to do as well. But I find that this has produced thoughts about the meaning of "holding in the Light" somewhat different from those

I expressed when I wrote the previous reflection on this phrase back in March. At that time, I wrote that holding in Light meant to ask God to be present with another, to give strength and comfort in a difficult situation, and for the other person to be aware of God's presence. While I still hold that view, I see it somewhat differently today.

I found myself asking if I can hold myself in the Light and, if so, what does that mean? The answer that came to me was yes. When I have found myself in difficult circumstances, I have asked God to be with me and to give me the strength I need to deal with the situation. In that sense, I am holding myself in the Light. But at the same time, I know I am trying to ask God to give me the strength to accept the situation, to find meaning and purpose in it, and to be able to overcome my fear and say, "thy will be done" and mean it. That's not easy, and I can't claim I've always been able to do that.

In holding myself in the Light, I try to remind myself that if I believe in God's presence and goodness (as I do), then there must be purpose and meaning and some sliver of good in all the experiences that come to me; all are gifts intended to help me along my spiritual journey. None are inherently good or bad; it's only our thinking, as Shakespeare reminds us, that makes them one or the other. So, if we have a choice, why not assume there is some good even if it's very hard to find? I know: easy to say, but extremely hard to do. However, we have no other choice. Holding ourselves in the light is both to ask for God's presence and to be willing to accept the outcome no matter what that may be.

On the other hand, when it comes to holding another in the Light, I think that trying to find meaning and purpose and good in a difficult situation is not our responsibility. Our task in those situations is the opposite: it is to see the difficulty for what it is and not pretend otherwise. It is to feel, to the extent we can, the pain and suffering another is experiencing and acknowledge that. It is not to be the optimistic one, saying, all will be well, but to moan and cry out, "Why him, God, why him?" In doing so, we shoulder some of the burden of the pain and try to unite with it, leaving the other person the task of finding whatever meaning, purpose, or good they can find in the situation.

While we can never experience the real pain and suffering of another or the mental anguish or fear, we can perhaps imagine it from some similar experience of our own or by imagining how we would feel in the same situation. And if we can do that, if we can enter into and experience the condition of another as if it were truly our own and still say "thy will be done," then the Light we hold another in will be imbued with real power—the power that comes from our confidence that God is with us at all times, the power that comes from the belief in God's goodness, the power of our love for another, and the power to accept all that life has to offer no matter how difficult it seems to our limited vision.

Dear friend, that is the Light I'm holding you in this morning.

Leaping into the Void

October 2020

Throughout the course of my life, I have found it easier to determine when there is a "leading" I am intended to follow than to determine when such a leading has ended and it's time or appropriate to lay it down. Such is the case with the writing of these reflections.

When I began writing in March 2020, it was clear this was something I was being called to do, something that was important for me to do for my own benefit and to share with others with whom I would not be having direct contact for some unforeseeable time. However, I assumed that the Covid-19 pandemic would end, in-person meetings for worship would resume, and I would return. That has not been the case. Consequently, I'm thrown back on my own devices, attempting to find a sign that says "continue" or "enough."

Many of the short essays I've written reflect a movement in my own spiritual journey that was going on even before the pandemic began. The pandemic and the necessity of meeting for worship alone provided a space that enabled those concerns to rise to the surface and were often reflected—although indirectly and perhaps apparent only to me—in many of the short essays I wrote. It seems quite clear now that a particular phase of my spiritual journey was coming to a close and that to be open to what might happen next, I need to be willing to give up some of the past to be empty enough to receive new leadings. *The Book of Runes* says it is time for me to make an "empty-handed leap into the void," and while that sounds overly dramatic, it also sounds right.

Two Meditations

ON THE INTRUSION OF THE DIVINE INTO MY DAILY LIFE

February 2022
Friends Journal

THE INTRUSION OF THE DIVINE into my daily life occurs when I am able to cease seeing myself as an entity separate and distinct from the world of creation in which I exist—when I can see myself, as if with a cosmic eye, as simply part of that world, no different or more significant than a rock, a tree, a squirrel, a bird, a fish, or a flower. In those moments a crack opens, small and thin, but large enough for God to rush in. Suddenly I find myself either empty and open to being filled, or so filled with God's presence that I am overwhelmed.

EMPTY

I walk through streets at night, alone, distracted by the cars, the buildings, the frustrations of the day, the fears and anxieties and constant preoccupation with what the future might or might not bring. Without my sensing it, the night air washes all that away, leaving behind a trail of abandoned thoughts and ideas, like dry leaves blown away by the wind. And then, empty at last, I look up and out to the night sky, black and limitless, out to the edges of eternity. In that moment you come to me; suddenly, swiftly, completely. You come like a lover, full of passion and joy, but full of peace as well. You come with the sound of tiny cymbals ringing in my ears, the sound of laughter in the night. And I, emptied at last of all desire but to be in unity with you, welcome you with outstretched arms. Your joy permeates my entire body until incomprehensibly, the vast universe before me and I are one. You in me, me in you, no bounds, no self, no other, no life, no death, no sorrow, no joy.

FULL

At low tide the edge of the waves is like a piece of lace thrown up on the sand and snatched away before the pattern can be deciphered. The waves break one hundred yards offshore, one right after another in steady succession. The rocks are black, with black shadows hardly distinguishable from the substance of the rocks themselves. At high tide the waves crash against them flinging foam into the air, covering rocks and shadows alike. The water is a white rolling foam surging over the beach and under the boardwalk. The sky is filled with stars, an orange moon hovers above the horizon. The moon is calm; the sea is raging.

I stand on the boardwalk and face the waves, ten feet high, racing towards me. The wind blows spray in my face, my clothes are drenched. I shout for joy, but my voice is lost in the sound of the surf breaking relentlessly on the shore. This is what it means to be alive: insignificant, powerless, alone with God.

(God is in the raging sea, in the breaking waves; God is in the thunder and in the rain, in the wind, and in the fire blazing. God is in the passion as well as in the peace.)

Sitting with Jesus 2

November 2021

During the week I supplement my hour of meeting for worship via Zoom on Sunday with daily meditation in a Catholic church near where I live that is open for an hour late in the afternoon. The church is huge; it must seat 1,000 people, but on weekday afternoons only two priests and I are present. Going there has once again made me think about the role of Jesus in my spiritual life and recall some of the experiences I've had envisioning him present and having a conversation with him as with a friend.

This approach to prayer began while I was attending a solitary spiritual retreat at Pendle Hill, the Quaker study center outside of Philadelphia. I was feeling particularly unhappy about almost everything in my life and decided to spend a week at Pendle Hill to see if I could re-energize myself. The week before I was due to go, there was a huge snowstorm. My car was embedded in four feet of snow, and I had some reservations about driving. But since Pendle Hill was only a half hour's drive from where I lived and once there my car would just sit for a week by which time the snow would probably have melted, I decided to proceed as planned.

When I got to Pendle Hill the entire campus was covered in a blanket of untrammeled white snow. Narrow roadways had been plowed through the drifts ending in parking lots surrounded by at least five feet of piled-up snow. Narrower walkways lined by low walls of snow connected one building to another. The snow gave the place an even greater sense of peace and serenity than was normally the case.

I had no plan for what I would do that week, other than spending time alone each day sitting in the meeting room and meditating on what I wanted to do at that point in my life. The first day I arrived I went to the library to look at reading lists for classes that were being offered, to see if I might want to sit in on one while I was there. A class about prayer attracted my attention. Prayer was something I had struggled with ever since giving up the habitual recitation of the Our Father and Hail Mary I had learned growing up as a Catholic. There were several books on the shelf for the class, so I browsed through a few, coming across one that discussed alternative forms of prayer. One idea interested me. It suggested imagining Jesus sitting in the room with you and having a conversation with him as you would with a friend. Jesus was still an important figure in my spiritual life, but I was having a hard time connecting with him so this seemed like an approach worth trying.

The following morning, I stayed in the meeting room by myself after meeting for worship had ended and everyone else had left for classes or Pendle Hill work. Another snowstorm had already begun. Through the few small windows in the meeting room, I could see snowflakes swirling in the air outside and sense the power of the storm. The storm kept everyone inside so few people came into the barn where the meeting room was, enhancing the solitude and silence. It was like being in the eye of a hurricane: outside the storm was raging, but I sat in its center in peace and calm.

Throughout the morning I envisioned Jesus sitting on the bench opposite me and slightly to the right. He looked like his usual self: long hair, beard, long robes, even sandals despite the snow. I described all the things that were bothering me and asked hypothetical questions, not expecting answers, and laughed out loud at myself when I said such things as, "What would you do, Jesus?" imitating a popular slogan that was going around at the time. Jesus sat silent, patiently listening, but his silence didn't bother me; it felt like a good exercise, and I enjoyed the idea of someone being there to keep me company even if only someone I imagined.

After lunch I returned to the meeting room and continued sitting in silence. I did not envision Jesus being present as consciously as I had in the morning, but from time to time I glanced over to the bench opposite me and he was still there, sitting in silent meditation as he had been all day. I no longer asked questions; I simply sat, enjoying the silence knowing I was sheltered in this place in the center of the storm which continued unabated. After a long period of silence in which I truly thought about nothing, he spoke. I use the word "spoke" deliberately because that is how it felt to me. It was not as if I heard something only in my mind; nor was it an audible voice that would have been heard by someone else sitting with me. But it seemed nonetheless that the words had been spoken aloud. "You are not alone," he said. That was all.

At that moment I felt like George Fox walking in the fields at night. Like Fox, I felt I had reached the point when "all my hopes . . . were gone so that I had nothing outwardly to help me, nor could I tell what to do, then, Oh then, I heard a voice which said, 'There is one Christ Jesus that can speak to thy condition.'" While Jesus did not answer any of the questions I had posed in the morning—in fact, his comment seemed irrelevant to my concerns—I knew almost immediately that what he said had gone to the heart of a fundamental issue of my life.

Throughout my childhood, as a teenager, a young adult and even into adulthood, my inner life was dominated by the feeling that I was alone, that there was no one I could really rely on, no one I could truly turn to for help, no one I could completely trust—not parents, not teachers, not friends. If I believed that God was with me, it was an intellectual belief, not something I truly felt. But when I heard those words I knew them to be true in a way I hadn't known before. They were a contradiction to my inner-most fear. They allowed me to realize that I had not been alone in the past and to see how God had been present and guiding me at critical moments in my life. That meant that God would be there in the future as well; that there was indeed someone I could trust, someone who would help and guide me, and whether that was God or Jesus or both didn't seem to matter.

By the end of the week an additional two feet of snow had fallen. I drove home without a clear idea of what I would do, but with the confident feeling that whatever I decided God, or Jesus—I still wasn't sure which—would be there to guide me. By the time I reached home I knew that if I wanted to find new meaning for my life, I had to stop doing the things that were making me unhappy. I had to close a door behind me if I wanted to give God the opportunity to open a door to a new path.

Remembering that experience while sitting in the church made me realize I was at a similar point in my life again. While previously the issue had been about my work—and deciding to close one door had in fact opened another to a new and more fulfilling experience—this time the issue was my spiritual life. That made me think about having a conversation with Jesus again, which in turn brought up the question of where he would sit, but this time in a very different way. What if I was not the one who decided where he would sit; what if he made that decision himself? This alone was a disturbing thought—a symbol of giving up control completely and letting him take charge.

As I pondered this idea, somewhat to my surprise Jesus arrived, uninvited you might say. He came down the side aisle to my left and into my pew, which meant there was no question about where he would sit. After he was seated, unlike in my previous imaginings when I envisioned him taking my hand, he calmly put his right arm around my shoulder. It was the type of affectionate gesture a father would make to a son, an elder brother to a younger one, or a best friend to a best friend. It had an immediate emotional impact on me. My father never offered me physical affection, I had no elder brother, and many of my male friends seemed wary of showing even the modest physical affection of a hug. The physical contact was something I had always longed for, and it felt as if Jesus once again knew what I needed to hear, or in this case feel, more than I did.

After a few minutes I allowed myself to relax and, in my imagination, rested my head upon his shoulder as one disciple is said to have done at the last supper. I felt a security and comfort I had seldom felt before and would have been content to remain like that for the whole hour. But soon he began to speak, and to speak at greater length than he had before, and I had to sit up to listen.

"It's time for you to go out on your own, John. I've taught you all I can, and I think you have a good understanding of what I've said. The time for studying is over; it's time to put what you've learned to use, and you can only do that on your own, I can't do that for you. But don't worry, I'll be here. I'll be looking forward to your coming back from time to time to tell me how things are going, and if you need advice or support of course I'm always available no matter where you are." He paused as if to let that all sink in.

"This may seem difficult but I'm confident you can do it." He reminded me how unprepared his disciples felt when he sent them out to preach. Don't worry, he told them; when the time comes God will tell you what to say. He was encouraging me to think the same would be true for me, but quite frankly I didn't believe him. I didn't think I was ready. I was comfortable sitting there with him beside me, comfortable thinking about his teachings intellectually. To get up and go out on my own was scary. I didn't think I had learned his lessons as well as he thought I had, and I often felt lost and alone. I'm not ready, was what I wanted to say, but he just sat there calmly smiling, rubbing my shoulder in a way that felt he was both reassuring me and gently pushing me forward in the same affectionate way a mother bird might use to prepare a baby bird to be ready to be pushed out of the nest.

"You remember the story of the man who gave each of his three servants talents to invest while he went away?" he asked. "Many people misunderstand that story because they associate the word talents, which meant money in my time, with the meaning of talent today—a skill, a gift of something you can do well. It's not a bad way to interpret the story, but there is another way to look at it. Two of the servants invested the money. They had no experience investing money and might have lost it as easily as made more. It was a risk, and the result of taking it was that they discovered something new about themselves that increased their self-confidence and pride. They also pleased their employer, not only because they made money but because they were self-confident enough to avail themselves of the opportunity he offered them. The third man was not. He revealed his lack of confidence in himself by holding on to the money. To grow, to become the person God created you to be, you must be willing to take risks. You must understand that the only failure in life is not trying; all else is simply a way of learning. So, which are you? Are you the one who is going to stay here sitting on this bench and never experience the greater wonder life has to offer you, or the one who is going to take the risk and discover something new about yourself and please God?"

Of course, he said none of this; it was all just my imagination. Yet at the same time, it was nothing I thought up on my own. The ideas came to me from another source and that source might just as well have been Jesus. I was very moved by what I imagined he said. It showed a real love for me and a hope that I would take the opportunity life was offering. Still, I hesitated. Then suddenly, he got up and walked away. I was so taken by surprise I wanted to call out, *Wait, where are you going?* I felt as abandoned as his disciples must have felt when he said he was leaving them and even more so after his death when they must have felt suddenly abandoned and uncertain what to do. Then

I heard his voice again: "Remember what I first told you," he said. And of course, I did.

When the time came for the church to close, I had to leave whether I wanted to or not. Once outside I paused at the top of the large flight of stairs that leads down to the sidewalk. The sky was already dark and a vast space stretching to eternity opened before me. Standing on the landing, I no longer felt the hesitation and uncertainty I had felt inside. I felt an unusual sense of joy and elation, much like I imagined a baby bird must feel perched on the edge of its nest ready to leap into the unknown for the first time. A passerby would have seen me standing there alone, but I knew that was not the case. Whether it was Jesus or God or both who were with me, I was not certain. But I heard someone whisper in my ear a word that was both command and invitation: FLY!

Accidents

December 2022

Although I'd been visiting Lancaster, PA, at least once a month for many months, I had never been able to attend meeting for worship at the Lancaster Friends Meeting. The meeting house seemed far away from the places where my partner and I usually stayed. In addition, we tried to leave Lancaster as early as we could on Sunday after he finished his work as the weekend psychiatrist at a local clinic. A meeting for worship ending at 11:30 plus a little socializing made that difficult, so it was easier to attend my usual meeting in Philadelphia via Zoom. But Labor Day weekend we were staying through Monday, so with no rush to leave on Sunday it was convenient for me to attend meeting for worship.

I'd been to the Lancaster meeting house many years before while taking a class on Quaker history, but had no recollection of its character. When I entered and sat down, I found it reminded me of the meeting room in the old Chestnut Hill Meeting House where I worshipped for many years. There were double-hung windows on three sides of the room, all open to a light breeze. There were traditional Quaker benches arranged in a square with an empty space in the center, but no fireplace, which was a distinctive feature of Chestnut Hill's meeting room.

Meeting for worship was uneventful. Several messages were offered, but none seemed particularly intended for me. That was fine. I don't expect insight and revelation every week. It was enjoyable enough to simply be able to attend meeting for worship in person, with real people, rather than staring at digital images on my computer screen. After meeting ended an older man offered to give me a ride back to my AirBnB, but he wanted to socialize first. That was also fine. Others, leaving earlier, offered me a ride instead, but I thought it was more polite to stick with the man who had made the first offer.

On the way he generously shared some facts about his life. He ended his story by saying, "My life has been an accident." Before I could ask him what he meant by that, we reached the street where I had to get off. Nor did I have the presence of mind to share my immediate reaction; as I was getting out, I should have simply said, "There are no accidents," leaving him with something to ponder just as his comment left me something to ponder in the coming weeks and led me to realize that this was the message I had been led to attend Lancaster Meeting to hear.

Accident is an interesting word. It can mean something unpleasant, like falling off a ladder and breaking a leg, or it can refer to something that has a positive outcome, just not the one that was intended. Both meanings have the same essential characteristics: both are unexpected, not planned, and neither is under our own control. Thinking about these two different meanings has made me wonder which meaning the man meant and served as a reminder of the definition that fits my experience and beliefs.

During the first half of my life, I considered certain events to be merely accidental or interesting coincidences. But when I became a Quaker and began to view my life from a spiritual perspective, I became convinced that this was not the case. I came to believe that each event was an example of God—or at least some aspect of the Divine Spirit—intervening in my life to guide me along a spiritual path. Nothing was just accidental; nothing was mere coincidence. Everything had meaning and purpose in relation to my spiritual journey. Even events that seemed minor and inconsequential often turned out to contain messages or be messengers providing me with guidance.

When I look at the description of Jesus's life in the gospels, everything appears accidental. He just seems to wander around from village to village bumping into people. Nothing is planned; everything is unexpected and none of it is under his own control. As he is leaving town, a rich young man comes up and asks about eternal life; as he's coming back from a journey, a Roman centurion suddenly appears and asks for help; he meets a blind man while walking on the road or a Samarian woman when he stops at a well to get a drink. He takes a morning walk in the temple and meets a man waiting by a healing pool. His life appears to be a series of accidental encounters that he uses as opportunities for teaching. But underneath all this apparent randomness, I believe his life conveys the same message found throughout his teachings.

Although Jesus never uses these words explicitly, a central feature of his teachings is placing your trust in God. When he says don't worry about what you'll eat or what you will wear; when he says behold the birds of the air who neither sow nor reap or take no concern for tomorrow—the underlying message in all these statements is trust that God will provide the resources you need. Jesus makes this point emphatically when he sends his followers out to preach. Take nothing with you, he says, but the clothes on your back. Not even an extra cloak. Don't worry about where you'll stay, and don't even worry about what to say: Trust that God will put the right words in your mouth when you need them.

This is the way Jesus leads his own life. He trusts that God will lead him to those places and experiences most appropriate to his spiritual journey, to the fulfilling of his purpose, his mission, in this life. As Isaac Penington put it, he has given up his own "willing," given up the notion that he is in control of his life. He sees each person he meets, each circumstance he finds himself in, as meaningful, all sent by God to lead him on his way. His task is simply to accept where he is led and to follow without reservations, without even knowing where the path might lead. This is the example Jesus sets; this is the challenge he presents to his audiences and to us. And when he says, "I am the way," I think he is referring to this unexpressed message behind what appears to be random wandering around.

Although we like to think we are in control of our lives, fundamentally we are not. God is a constant presence, whether we perceive that or not. We are being guided along a path designed specifically and uniquely for each of us that will allow each of us to fulfill our purpose and achieve the most spiritual growth possible in this lifetime. The difference between Jesus and each of us is that he was able to consciously accept that idea, to consciously give up his own "willing," while we continue to think we are in control of our destiny.

I wish I had taken the time to say to the man who gave me a ride, I once thought my life was an accident, too, but I've come to believe that there are no "accidents" just as I believe there are no coincidences; everything is purposeful, everything has meaning, everything contributes to my—and your—spiritual journey. If we are truly willing to trust that God is leading our life, each accident, whether it appears to be positive or negative, has within it a gift if our hearts are open to receive it.

Welcoming Temptation

February 2023
Friends Journal

THE PRAYER THAT Jesus taught the crowds in Matthew 6:9–13 and his disciples in Luke 11:2–4—the one referred to as the "Our Father" when I learned it as a child—contains the phrase "lead us not into temptation" in the King James Version. This has always struck me as a strange phrase, implying that without such a prayer God *would* lead us into temptation. Why would God do that, since everyone knows that temptations are things to be avoided, invitations to do something wrong or forbidden. Or are they?

A clue to the answer to this question seems to me to lie in the story of Jesus's temptation in the wilderness after his baptism by John. This incident was obviously important since it is included in each of the three synoptic gospels—Mark, Matthew, and Luke—in almost the same mystical terms: the Spirit descends like a dove and the voice of God is heard. I often wonder how the gospel writers knew some of the stories they wrote down. In the case of his baptism and subsequent experience, no one would have known about them except Jesus himself. For the gospel writers to have known the story, Jesus would have had to tell it to someone else, then that person tell it to another and so forth until it was finally written down. Then copied or rewritten and embellished by the gospel writer decades later.

Although we cannot know how Jesus might have described these experiences himself, I believe it is possible to tell the story of his temptation in a non-mystical way that is consistent with the intent of the gospel versions and makes the story relevant to each of us today, by suggesting an understanding of the meaning and purpose of temptations that differs from the usual one.

My version goes like this: As far as his community is concerned, Jesus has led an exemplary life. He has looked after his mother and his brothers and sisters, helped others in Nazareth, and followed all the Jewish spiritual and social practices. Nonetheless, he feels something is missing; he feels called to be doing something different with his life, but he's not certain what that is. He is impressed by what he hears about John's preaching and goes to be baptized with the hope that the experience will help him know what to do. He is thirty years old; his brothers and sisters are old enough to take care of themselves and their mother; he is dissatisfied with his life and ready to change.

In that frame of mind, he comes to the Jordan and is baptized—submerged fully in the cool "living" river water at the hands of John. When Jesus emerges from under the water, he feels energized in a way he has never felt before. It is both an emotionally and spiritually inspiring experience, equivalent to feeling that he has been born anew, as he will later say, with a stronger awareness of God's presence in his life. Although he may not know why he feels this way, the feeling is so intense he cannot simply turn around and go home, nor can he stay around and hang out with the crowd. In Mark's gospel it says the spirit "driveth" him into the wilderness (Mark 1:12), while others say "led" or "guided." I prefer the word "driveth" because it implies that the impetus to flee the crowd and be alone was so strong, he could not resist.

None of this seems unusual to me. Many people have had strong conversion experiences in which the presence of God is felt suddenly and more intensely than before. And often this is accompanied by the feeling of needing to be alone to assimilate the experience. On a more modest scale, I have had similar feelings after unexpectedly delivering a personally moving message in Quaker meeting for worship. Elsewhere I have written that the experience is like that of a tree shaking in the aftermath of a hurricane, so overwhelming is the feeling of being used or inspired by God. Afterwards, I do not want to talk to anyone; I want to quickly leave and be alone.

Since it is the "Spirit" that drives Jesus into the wilderness, it must be the same Spirit that at his baptism descended on him like a dove, the Spirit of God. If that is the case, it would seem reasonable to assume that the Spirit did this to continue to nurture him and help him understand the meaning of his experience. But that is not what appears to happen. Instead, Jesus is tempted, and since it is said that he is tempted by Satan the implication is that he is being lured to do something wrong. It isn't necessary to believe in Satan to understand what Jesus's temptations might have been. Having experienced a surge of energy and a calling much stronger than anything he's previously experienced, it seems natural that he would wonder what he should do in response. Does it mean he should become a leader of the Jewish people's efforts to overthrow the oppression of the Romans? Does it mean he should use his abilities in a way that will bring prosperity to himself and his family? Should he seek material success, prestige, leadership in the world? To each of the three temptations he is offered he says no, but there is nothing to which he says yes.

There is, however, another way of looking at this experience. If it is the Spirit of God that leads him into the wilderness, we must assume that whatever happens to him there is positive—something that will help him understand his baptismal experience and find his way forward—for God is good and brings only good things into our lives. So, although the word temptation normally has a negative connotation, in this instance it has a different meaning.

My *Oxford American Dictionary* gives "to make a trial of" or "to try the resources of" as alternative definitions of *tempt* or *temptations*. To put it simply, it means "to be tested." In fact, this is the sense of the story given by David Bentley Hart's recent translation of the gospels that tries to be faithful to the original Greek. He translates the phrase in the Lord's Prayer as "not bring us trial." From this perspective, the temptations aren't negative at all, and they do not come from Satan. They come from God and are tests to determine if Jesus is ready to commit himself to a spiritual path by testing whether he is strong enough to say no to other directions for his life. They provide an opportunity for Jesus to make conscious decisions about the way he wants to live his life and the person he wants to be. They are a test of his integrity—his commitment to follow his spiritual values—and of his faith that God, and not he, is guiding his life.

One of the important lessons of the story is the understanding that it is often necessary to say no to some paths to find the one most conducive to the evolution of our spiritual journey. Sometimes it is necessary to close the door on one set of interests or activities to give God the opportunity to open the door to another. Although Jesus leaves the wilderness with no clarity about what he should do, saying no to the temptations was an essential step in his spiritual journey, one that closed off certain options and prepared him to be ready to say yes when the appropriate direction presented itself.

Jesus returns to Nazareth: In some versions, it says he learns that John has been imprisoned and his preaching silenced. This itself must pose a question for Jesus: should he take over in John's place.

In another version, he goes to the synagogue and is given the scroll of Isaiah to read.

> *When he opened the book, he found the place where it was written, The Spirit of the Lord is upon me, because he*

has anointed me to preach the gospel to the poor. (Luke 4:17–18)

The words find him; he does not select them. It is the voice of God speaking directly to him and in that moment, he realizes what he is meant to do, what he is to say yes to. When he says to those assembled, "This day this scripture is fulfilled in your ears" (Luke 4:21), he is saying it to himself for the first time: *Today, right now, I know what God is calling me to do and I am ready.*

Temptations come in many different forms. Some seem so minor and insignificant that indulging in them doesn't seem to do any harm. But each one, no matter how insignificant it may seem, is a test of our integrity—our ability to make conscious decisions about how and by what standards we want to live our lives—and a test of our faith in God's goodness and that it is God who is guiding our lives.

There have been many times in my life when I was tempted to pursue a certain direction and the ability to say no enabled me to be open to an unexpected and more appropriate opportunity. At one point in my career, I was being considered for the position of dean of the architecture school where I was teaching in Austin, Texas. It was a position I thought I wanted and eagerly sought. During that time, I came to a convention in Philadelphia where I happened "by chance" to bump into the dean of the University of Pennsylvania's architecture school. He said he knew of my situation and advised me not to take the position, not to get bogged down in academic administration. For me, his words were equivalent to the words of Isaiah for Jesus. I knew immediately that he was right. I knew it was my ego that had wanted the position for the recognition, and it was not something consistent with my real interests. Upon returning to Austin, I withdrew my name from consideration. Shortly thereafter, I was approached by a representative of the mayor of Philadelphia asking me if I would take the position of director of the city's housing and community development programs—a job much more consistent with my interests and values, and one I would not have been able to say yes to if I had not said no to the other. Closing one door had given God the opportunity to open another.

Jesus did not fear the temptations he faced in the wilderness; indeed, I imagine he welcomed them, knowing they were merely a test of his integrity and faith, an essential step in the process of finding the path God was calling him to follow. So too we should not fear temptations, but rather welcome them as opportunities to demonstrate our consistent commitment to following a spiritual path and letting God lead our lives. Then, perhaps, we might offer the following prayer in lieu of the phrase Matthew and Luke suggest:

Our Father, Divine Intelligent Energy of the Universe, give us the strength to resist the paths that would lead us astray, and help us to recognize the ones most conducive to progress on our spiritual journey.

Enjoy Your Life

April 2023

The path I walk along on my morning walk is now lined with beds of daffodils in bloom. Most of them are pale white; some have an orange center—that part of the flower that looks like an ornate brass musical instrument—and some are the bright yellow color traditionally associated with daffodils. They are beautiful and inspiring so on my way back to my apartment I pick a few that are here in a colorful vase on my desk while I write.

The flowers remind me of a story in Alexander Lowen's book, *Joy*. I like this story so much I'm going to quote it rather than paraphrasing it.

> *When my son was about five years old, I made an effort to get him to go to Sunday School. My argument was that he would learn about God. He said I know about God. When I asked him what he knew he pointed to some flowers that were growing in the garden near where he was standing and replied, 'He is there.' I sensed that he had a feeling about God which was more important than what he could learn in school, and I abandoned my effort to get him to go to Sunday School. I felt sure that if he was aware that God was in the flowers, he also knew that God was in his own body too.*

I was surprised that Lowen, a prominent psychiatrist and founder of the bioenergetic method of psychotherapy, believed that there was that of God in every person. That seems to qualify him to be an honorary member of the Religious Society of Friends, along with my old friend Marcus Aurelius.

Yes, there is that of God in the flowers as well as in us human beings. And that thought makes me wonder what definition of "God" would fit both the flowers and us. "Father" doesn't seem right, and while I'm comfortable with the Inner Light as a term applicable to humans, I'm not so sure I can as easily apply it to the rest of creation. Which reminds me that "Creator" seems to work, as might "Great Spirit" or other terms without human connotations. Native Americans and other indigenous peoples—and Hindus too, Lowen says—believe there is the presence of God in all creation, a belief many in today's world seemed to have lost.

My walk takes me past the daffodils to a point where I turn to go into the mini forest along the railroad tracks I mentioned in an earlier reflection. At this point there is a small playground surrounded by a chain-link fence. Within the fenced-in area there are only two pieces of playground equipment: a jungle gym to climb on and a set of swings. Today only two people were there, who I assumed were a mother and her daughter. The daughter, probably about eight years old, was dressed liked she might have been a fairy godmother in a play or ballet if she had a wand to wave. Her white skirt came to about her knees with glitter all over it that sparkled in the sunlight. Her blouse was rose-colored, with long, loose sleeves. The only element out of character were the running shoes she wore instead of ballet slippers. She was running in circles around the playground equipment, with arms outstretched as if she was expecting to take off and fly at any moment. Her long sleeves billowed in the wind she created by her movement as round and round she went while her mother sat on a swing, silently smiling as she watched her daughter's obvious joy.

Many people have observed that for young children, the line between their spiritual nature and their "human nature" is very thin and easily crossed. If there is a Light Within, present from birth, then young children seem to have a natural, unselfconscious connection to it that is expressed in the sheer joy of living. As we grow older and are required to take on the responsibilities of adult life, we appear to lose this easy connection to our spiritual nature. Then, the Light Within may appear to have grown dim, but that is not the case. It is always glowing with the same intensity, waiting for us to pull back the veils and let it shine. It is no wonder Jesus said that as adults we must be born again and become as little children if we wish to fully enter the Kingdom of God.

The young girl's Light was shining brightly this morning, sending out beams of energy—for light is energy—that transformed her, brought her joy, and enabled her to let the presence of God flow through her and transmit that joy to her mother, myself, and anyone else who happened to see her. This sense of joy and boundless energy made me think that the best definition of "God"—the one that fits both the flowers and each of us—might be exactly that: a divine intelligent energy that permeates the universe and everything within it, an energy that propels the bulb to become the daffodil, the caterpillar to become the butterfly, and each of us to strive to reach the full realization of "that of God" within us.

Leading a spiritual life is often portrayed as something hard to do and one that requires giving up all that is pleasant in life. Early Quakers thought music, art, sports—almost anything that gave pleasure, it seems—were a distraction from a spiritual life. But it should be remembered that Jesus attended banquets, drank wine with friends, and enjoyed his life. If the Inner Light is glowing, then there must be joy in the pleasure of being alive and experiencing the wonder of creation. And so, with that thought in mind, I leave you with a few words of advice I wrote recently for myself that may be appropriate for you as well.

Enjoy your life.
Do a little work each day, but not too much.
just enough to know you still have
something to contribute to the world.
Do a little singing, a little dancing, a little praying,
to show the Great Spirit
you are grateful for its wonderful gifts.

Do a little writing, without worrying
whether it will lead to anything.
Just share some thoughts to leave behind
for those who follow.
Try to do something nice for at least one person each day,
for more if possible.
Sit outside and enjoy the sun, the songs of birds,
the trees and flowers, the sky, the clouds, the breeze.
Enjoy your life.

The Life of the Spirit

April 2023
Friends Journal

WHENEVER SOMEONE I am meeting for the first time asks, "who are you" or something similar, I'm tempted to say, "I am a spiritual being enjoying an earthly experience." It's a clever phrase, not original with me but one with which I'm generally comfortable. However, I recently realized that I've never thought deeply about what it means; that is, until a photograph from Duane Michals's sequence *The Spirit Leaves the Body* (1968) caught my attention. I've long been an admirer of Duane Michals's work and this sequence of seven photographs has been one of my favorites. But like the phrase about being a spiritual being, I had never thought deeply about the ideas implied by this sequence of photographs. My reflection on the photographs has led me to a better understanding of what it means to be a spiritual being and has enabled me to order miscellaneous ideas I've thought, read, and even written about over the years. My realization was like what happens when the last turn of a kaleidoscope brings all the chaotic pieces of glass into a beautiful and coherent pattern. It has also led me to a new understanding of the Quaker concept of the Inner Light and the purpose of silent worship, which I find truer to my experience and more helpful to understanding my spiritual journey.

THE PHOTOGRAPHS

There are seven photographs in *The Spirit Leaves the Body* sequence. The first and last appear to be the same; they show the body of an old and frail man lying naked on a bed or a cloth-covered platform. In between these two are five other photographs that show the transparent figure of a ghost-like younger man superimposed on the image of the man lying on the bed. In the first, the transparent man is sitting up; then, in the next he's sitting on the edge of the bed (my favorite photograph in the series and the one the prompted these reflections);

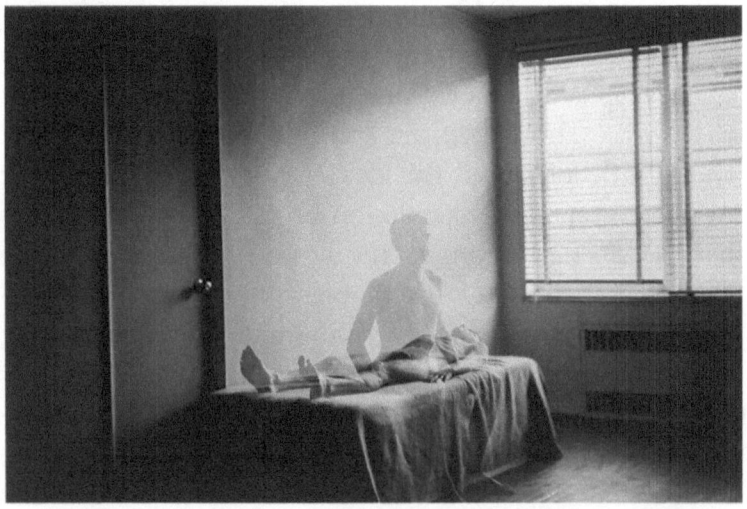

Duane Michals, *The Spirit Leaves the Body*, 1968

then he's moving toward the camera and becoming more transparent until he finally disappears. There are neither captions nor text, as there often are in other sequences of Michals's work. We are left to figure out the meaning on our own.

The sequence suggests that each of us is composed of both body and spirit, a belief that permeates much of Michals's work and one I share. The question this particular sequence poses is this: Is the man in the first photograph alive or dead? You may not believe there is a spirit at all, in which case this question is irrelevant. And even if you do believe, you may still think the question irrelevant—after all, when you're dead you're dead; what difference does it make when the Spirit leaves the body? However, I think the answer to that question is key to how I view my life (and how to view yours) and how I view my death.

The second chapter of Genesis tells us that God created a human being from dust and then breathed into this inanimate object, thereby bringing it to life. I understand that the Hebrew word for "breath" can also mean "Spirit." So that implies that God transferred some of Its Spirit, Its likeness, to the human figure, and as a result there is "that of God" in each person. Whether I believe this is literally the way life began is not important; it's the spiritual concept that interests me. If at birth (and I don't want to get into a discussion of exactly at what point I mean) the Spirit gives life to the body, then what happens at death? Does the body wear out, collapse, die, and then the Spirit leaves? Or does the Spirit leave either of its own accord—or called back by God—and having done so, having removed the source that originally gave life to the inanimate body, does the body then die? If I consider myself to be a spiritual being having an earthly experience the answer is clear: The spirit leaves and then the body, no longer needed, dies. Consequently, in the first photograph, the man is alive; in the last he is dead. This understanding is what gives rise to my concept of what it means to be a spiritual being and what that means about my life and my death.

THE CONCEPT

The Spirit, being an aspect of God, never dies. It is eternal as God is eternal. It passes from one body to the next, from one lifetime to the next, and comes into each with a specific purpose and a plan to achieve that purpose. Both the purpose and the means by which it will be accomplished—everything from the selection of our parents to the events we will experience and the people we will come in contact with—are determined before birth and ingrained in our subconscious. Likewise, the knowledge of how to make our bodies function, our consciousness, and so much else is embedded subconsciously in our DNA and in other ways we have yet to understand. There are no coincidences; nothing we experience is accidental; everything is purposeful. But because the knowledge of our purpose and plan are in our subconscious, we do not remember them ourselves. Instead, we are given two guides: one is what we as

Quakers refer to as an Inner Light and the other, to be complimentary, might be called an Outer Light, similar to the "Light" we mean when we say we are holding someone "in the Light."

Both are guides; both have been entrusted with all the details of our purpose and plan, but each guides us in a different way. The Inner Light helps us to recognize the people and events that will lead us along the path that will provide the most spiritual growth we can achieve in this lifetime. The Outer Light leads us to the circumstances in which those people and events will appear.

How it does this I do not know, but that it does I am certain from the experiences of my own life. I know I have never made a decision about any aspect of my life; all decisions have been made by some outside force, by the unexpected influence of people and events that appear by "coincidence" in my life at just the right moment and are really messengers sent to guide me on my way. My task is simply to recognize and accept the guidance I am given and follow the paths on which I am led without necessarily knowing why or to what end. (If you think this idea is crazy, look at your own life. How many decisions have you actually made yourself; how many have been determined by the unexpected and "coincidental" influence of other people and events.) But both Inner and Outer Light are merely guides; we are free to follow or reject their guidance as we please; the only consequence is that we will have to try to learn those lessons again in another lifetime.

THE PURPOSE

In a general sense, the purpose of each lifetime is simply to advance along the path of spiritual growth. You might say it is analogous to the experience of being a student in school. You start in one grade and gain knowledge (one lifetime) then take the summer off (death) and then return to a higher grade (next lifetime) where you learn higher knowledge, proceeding along this alternating path until you have mastered all the subjects and graduate. What are we as spiritual beings learning in these successive lifetimes on earth? I believe we are learning to perfect our spirit's ability to love all creation unconditionally. Earth is our school, our learning laboratory, and the pleasures and desires of material existence are the deliberate means chosen for us before birth to help us develop the strength to overcome self-centeredness. Each aspect of our life provides a different kind of learning experience to enable us to perfect our ability to love unconditionally in all circumstances, with all people, and under all conditions.

THE INNER LIGHT
AND SILENT WORSHIP

All this brings me back to the concept of the Inner Light and the significance of silent worship. Historically, and even today, turning to the Inner Light for guidance is a core concept of Friends, almost as if that Light only comes on when we turn to it for assistance. But this is a misunderstanding; the Light is always on; we are always being guided in the direction of spiritual growth by both an Inner and an Outer Light. There is no need to ask for guidance. The problem is we are so distracted by our own concerns, our own needs, and desires, that we are not sufficiently awake and alert enough to see or recognize the guidance we are being given except in rare moments. Our task is to remove these blinders, to be awake (which is the way Buddha described himself to the first person he met after his enlightenment).

The purpose of silent meeting for worship is to help us do exactly that: to learn to turn off the distractions, the constant self-absorption we have with our own ideas, needs, and desires; and to awaken ourselves to an awareness of the presence of God in our lives. When we can do that in meeting for worship, we often hear a message from within or from another person that gives a new insight. But to hear that message we must be awake and alert, undistracted by our own thinking. We must give up "our own willing," as Isaac Pennington said, and be willing to accept the guidance we are given, the paths the Light illuminates. As I wrote in an early *Friends Journal* essay ["Wait and Watch," *FJ* June 2006], meeting for worship is about spiritual practice; it is an opportunity to learn how to be awake and alert so that in our daily lives the unobstructed Inner Light is able to help us recognize, hear, see, and accept the messages that come to us through the people and events that the Outer Light brings to guide us on our way. Rumi expresses this beautifully in the poem *The Guest House*, the last verse of which is, "Be grateful for whoever [or whatever] comes / because each has been sent as a guide from beyond."

DEATH

Death is not to be feared. Death is neither an end nor a final going home to God; it is a temporary visit, a brief summer vacation, before the spirit returns to the learning laboratory of earthly life to undertake the next lessons that will eventually lead it to perfection, to graduation, and to merger with the Divine Intelligent Energy of the Universe (my definition of the word God) and to new non-earthly experiences likely to be more wonderful than we can imagine.

To Err is Human;
To Forgive is Human Too

January 2024
Friends Journal

Each morning before I begin my day's activities, I say a prayer primarily of thanks for all the gifts and blessings I've received. However, it also includes the sentence, "Forgive me for all the things I have done in thought, word, and deed, that have hurt or offended others; let them forgive me, let me forgive those who have hurt or offended me, let me forgive myself." I've said this prayer, and consequently this sentence, so often and for such a long time that I now say it by rote without giving much thought to what the words mean for my daily spiritual life. So, when my computer calendar informed me that the coming Monday (September 23, 2023) was Yom Kippur, the day that Jewish people are expected to pray to God for forgiveness of their sins, I decided it would be good for me to spend the day thinking about forgiveness, which I did with surprising and unexpected results.

Whenever I begin to think about a spiritual issue, I first turn to the gospels to see what Jesus of Nazareth had to say. My sentence includes four aspects of forgiveness and so it was advice for each that I went seeking. I was surprised to find that the words "forgive" and "forgiveness" do not occur often and that the sayings or stories that were most helpful to me didn't include those words at all.

SEEKING GOD'S FORGIVENESS

My prayer is addressed to God, so the opening phrase—"forgive me for all that I have done"—is a request for God's forgiveness. Although this seemed like an appropriate request (perhaps influenced by my Catholic upbringing and years of going to confession to ask forgiveness for my sins), I was surprised to realize that it was incompatible with my concept of God and with the gospel story that speaks most clearly to me about God's forgiveness.

My concept of God is not an entity with human emotions or characteristics. It is more like an intelligent energy that is the source of and permeates all creation. Nonetheless, I believe that whatever it is for which we use the word God, it has a positive regard for all creation, including us human beings. In human language this positive regard is called "unconditional love" and I believe that is an accurate phrase: God's love is unconditional, unchanging, and bestowed on all equally, no matter what we do.

The story in the gospel that speaks most clearly to me about forgiveness and exemplifies the idea of God's unconditional love is the one called "the prodigal son."

(Luke 15:11–32) Like many others, I believe this parable is inappropriately named; it is really about a father and his relationship to his two sons. Some people view the story as an analogy for God's relation to human beings: the father stands for God, the sons for us. Although I don't read the story that way, I believe the father is a man living in the Kingdom of God, and as such, behaves in a way that manifests the presence of God in his life.

You will recall that the younger son asks for the share of his father's estate that he will inherit, he receives it, and then goes off and squanders it in what the gospel calls "wanton living." (Another way of looking at it is that he goes off and has fun and enjoys himself.) When the money runs out he decides to return home and rehearses a speech asking for forgiveness. But even before he can get the words out, his father welcomes him with open arms, gives him a ring and a robe, and organizes a party. The father's love for his son is unchanged; it is the same love that led him to give the resources. He placed no conditions on the gift of those resources; consequently, what his son did while he was away is of no concern to him. He does not judge his son's behavior; he loves him regardless of what he has done, which is to say he loves him unconditionally.

The same is true for God. The gift of life comes with no conditions attached. Nor does God judge our deeds as "good" or "bad." In God's eyes nothing is good or bad; it is, as Shakespeare reminds us, our own thinking that makes it so. The only thing God or the father might say is, what did you learn from that experience?

So, if God's love for me is unconditional, unchanging, and non-judgmental, why am I asking God for forgiveness? Indeed, it almost seems inappropriate and even insulting to ask for God's forgiveness as if it might not be given unless I asked. My best guess at the moment is that I am doing this to remind myself that my behavior often falls short of the spiritually-led person I want to be, and that acknowledgment helps me to see both the need and the way to change. While those insights are useful, a more appropriate prayer would be one that gives thanks to God for Its unconditional love despite my frequent failures to live up to the standards of the person I want to be.

SEEKING FORGIVENESS FOR HURTING OR OFFENDING OTHERS

The gospel gives quite clear advice when it comes to seeking forgiveness from those I've hurt or offended. In Matthew 5:23–24 Jesus says, "Therefore if thou bring thy gift to the altar and there rememberest that thy brother has ought against thee; leave there thy gift before the altar and go thy way; first be reconciled to thy brother, and then come and offer thy gift." This sentence contains three important ideas. The first is the meaning of the word "brother" (which I understand to mean sister, too). Jesus defines this word elsewhere (Luke 8:21) when he says my brothers "are those which hear the word of God and do it." A "brother" is both male and female, someone with whom you share something important in common and with whom you have a relationship that is even of higher priority than bringing a gift to the altar, which must have been a very important act for the Jewish people of the time.

The second thing the passage tells us is that if you know someone feels you have hurt or offended them, it is your responsibility to take the initiative to repair the damage done—whether or not you feel you have done something wrong. So long as your brother feels hurt, your relationship is broken and you must address it. The third thing the passage tells us is how to do that.

It is significant that the word used is "reconcile" and not the phrase "ask for forgiveness." Reconcile means to restore harmony to a relationship. How do you do that? By acknowledging what you did and apologizing for it. The focus of your action is on the feelings of the other party, relieving him or her of the burden of anger and resentment he or she may be carrying, a burden that can affect physical as well as spiritual well-being. There is a tendency to want to add the phrase "Please forgive me" or something similar. But I think that is inappropriate, and the reason that the saying uses the word reconcile.

In the TV series *The Tudors*, Charles Brandon is King Henry VIII's best friend. He travels to Scotland where he previously led a military campaign and meets the ghost of a man he killed. When he asks for forgiveness, the ghost says no; "You living are so selfish." To ask for forgiveness is a selfish act; it is concerned with relieving your shame and guilt for what you have done, whereas the focus of an apology should be on relieving the feelings of hurt of the person injured. If forgiveness is offered, it must be the voluntary decision of the other, and if it is withheld until your future actions show changed behavior, that is reasonable and appropriate too.

Certainly, relieving your guilt or shame is one of the benefits of reconciling with your brother. It may even be that guilt and shame, rather than your brother's anger, are the impetus for your action. Nonetheless, this is secondary to the primary objective of relieving your brother (or sister) of the burden they may still carry.

FORGIVING THOSE WHO HAVE HURT OR OFFENDED ME

The gospels have much to say about forgiving others. Perhaps the best-known example is in the Lord's Prayer. When I was growing up in the Catholic Church the phrase was "forgive us our trespasses as we forgive them that trespass against us." Current translations say the word is "debts," not "trespasses," and the phrase that follows is "as we *have forgiven* our debtors." In many other places we are told that unless we forgive others, God will not forgive us (Mark 11:25–26, Matthew 6:14–15, Luke 6:37). This seems to be a misunderstanding of the nature of God, as I previously discussed, and a lack of understanding of God's unconditional love. In addition, it too seems selfish; it is a kind of reciprocal forgiveness, a *quid pro quo* that has as its primary objective seeking forgiveness for myself and relief of my guilt and shame. Just as apologizing is intended to ease the burden of anger and resentment for someone else, so giving forgiveness should be for easing the burden of guilt and shame that another may feel as a result of their actions.

Most of the books or articles I've read about forgiving others emphasize the way in which such forgiveness releases our resentments and a constant inclination to relive the past. While this an important benefit, it also seems selfish. Forgiveness for me is an act of compassion—compassion for another and for the feelings they may have about actions they now regret. If, when apologizing for my actions, I hope for reconciliation, then when someone apologizes to me, I must be willing to be reconciled and help relieve the burdens they still carry.

Better, but more difficult, advice about forgiving others is given in Matthew 18:21–22 when Peter asks, "Lord, how oft shall my brother sin against me and I forgive him? Till seven times? Jesus saith unto him, I say not unto thee, Until seven times, but Until seventy times seven." By using the word "brother," the story is once again referring to someone with whom you have a relationship based on a common bond. A modern-day psychologist would say that to forgive someone who has hurt you seven times, much less 490 times, makes no sense; it would only encourage continued bad behavior knowing there would be no consequences. But much of what Jesus says doesn't make sense to people who are not living in the Kingdom of God. Here he is making the same point as before: Such relationships are of great importance, and you must do more than might reasonably be expected to maintain them.

When I think of someone who has hurt me and who I need to forgive, the first person who comes to mind is my father. He did not do me any physical harm or harshly criticize me; the harm he caused was purely psychological. He was an emotionally distant man and never expressed his feelings in words or obvious actions. He seemed indifferent to me, which I took as a lack of love. As a result, I developed a strong resentment toward him that was an expression of the disappointment I kept hidden within me. The phrase I've used is that I "hardened my heart against him." I said to myself, if you won't love me, I won't love you and thought that would be a form of punishment. Nelson Mandela, and many others, have referred to this type of resentment as taking poison with the belief that it will kill your enemy. The only one who gets hurt is yourself, and that was true for me. Once you harden your heart to someone, it becomes easy to harden your heart to others—and a hardened heart cannot express love, accept love from others, or be aware of God's love.

Unfortunately, I carried that same pattern into other relationships as an adult. When, on Yom Kippur, I thought about all the people who had hurt me, and all the grudges and resentments I still carried, I realized for the first time that none of them had intended to hurt me. It was my interpretation of their actions that caused the pain and suffering I experienced. It was merely my ego that was bruised, and no harm was actually intended or inflicted. It is true that in each situation there was some small incident that was the basis for my response, but it was minor and not intended to hurt. While I may have needed to forgive my father and others for those incidents, I suddenly realized the person I really needed to forgive was myself for thinking unfairly of them, and for the pain and suffering I caused myself by the resentment I created by my mistaken interpretation.

FORGIVING MYSELF

At the end of my day of reflection I came to see—much to my surprise—that forgiving myself was at the heart of my ability to achieve peace with myself for my actions and peace with others for theirs. The challenge was not to seek forgiveness externally, but to be able to extend to myself the same unconditional love God extends to me and that I am encouraged to extend to others. Unconditional love means accepting myself as I am, forgiving myself for my mistakes, and trying to learn from them. The same is true for others. Reconciling with someone I've injured is not sufficient unless I can also forgive myself; reconciling with someone who has injured me is not sufficient unless I can forgive myself for my resentment, including the way I might have created it myself by attributing to them something that wasn't there.

The actions for which I felt I needed to seek forgiveness, and the hurts I felt I needed to forgive, were all in the past. Consequently, it seemed that praying for forgiveness—from God, from others or for myself—is not as appropriate as praying for help in being able to extend unconditional love to everyone in my life and thereby making apology and forgiveness unnecessary. While I still feel it is good to ask for God's forgiveness as a reminder that I am not perfect, it seems more important to thank God for Its unconditional love and ask help in extending that to others. Consequently, I have revised my morning prayer to reflect this new perspective.

The title of the essay is altered from a quotation from Alexander Pope: "To err is human, to forgive divine." Pope's phrase implies that only God can truly forgive. However, I think it means that when we forgive others and ourselves, we come as close as we can in this lifetime to manifesting God's unconditional love. Forgiveness is the means; unconditional love is the goal.

Two Practical Commandments

January 2024

WHEN MY PARTNER was preparing to go on his first pilgrimage to Mecca, his father—who is a very devout Muslim—gave him two pieces of advice. First, do not complain. Second, assist others as much as you can.

There are two types of pilgrimages to Mecca. Umrah is the personal pilgrimage that can be performed in a single day any time of the year. It currently attracts over 100,000 people each day. The Hajj is the pilgrimage required of all Muslims who are capable of making it. It takes five to six days, occurs only at a specific time each year, and currently attracts over one million people each year from all parts of the world. Prior to Covid-19, it used to attract three million people. With such an enormous number of people concentrated in the same area, speaking different languages, trying to go to the same places and complete the same rituals, there is ample opportunity for problems to arise and consequently much that would be easy to complain about. But his father reminded him that to be able to undertake the pilgrimage at all is a privilege. Muslims believe that you do not *decide* to undertake the Hajj, you are *invited* and the one extending the invitation is God,

Allah. Therefore, to complain is to show disrespect and a lack of gratitude to God (Allah) for the privilege you have been granted.

Many people who attend the pilgrimage need assistance: Older people need to be pushed in wheelchairs from one location to another; others need help finding the tent they have been assigned to stay in amid thousands of tents; some have spent their life's savings just to get there and have no money left for food. Assisting others is a special spiritual duty and one that is a way of expressing gratitude to God (Allah).

But the qualifying phrase—*as much as you can*—has two important implications. It is first of all encouragement to do more than you might normally do to help others in your daily life. At the same time, it implies a limit: Do not be so focused on helping others, important as that is, that you neglect your own spiritual purposes. As much as you can, but not more.

This advice reminded me of the advice Jesus gives a man who asked him what to do to gain eternal life. He suggests that the man should follow two commandments: love God and love your neighbor as yourself (Matthew 22:37–39). I have difficulty understanding the meaning of the word "love" when applied to such an abstract entity as "God." A more understandable word or phrase that conveys the same intention for me, but in terms I can understand, is being grateful or giving thanks—thanks for the gift of life, for the privilege of being alive and living on such a wonderful and beautiful place as earth. The converse of being grateful—of expressing thanks—is complaining. Thus, my partner's father's advice seems to me to be a practical interpretation of the first commandment Jesus cites. This reminds me of a prayer attributed to an anonymous Benedictine nun: *Thank you for everything. I have no complaints.*

I have similar difficulty understanding the meaning of the word "love" when it comes to my neighbor. The parable of the Good Samaritan Jesus tells makes it clear that love in Jesus's view is not an emotional feeling but an action: assisting someone—anyone—in need. So here too, my partner's father's advice is essentially the same as the second commandment Jesus cites, only stated again in practical terms. But the commandment Jesus cites also has a qualifying phrase: "as yourself."

These two words seem to me to have a similar meaning to the phrase "as much as you can." Your commitment to assisting others, no matter how important that is, should not result in your neglecting to love yourself, that is, to give appropriate attention to your own spiritual purposes. There is a natural tendency to focus on our own needs and desires, our own spiritual goals, so there is good reason why both statements place helping others first as a way to emphasize the importance of that activity.

**Do not complain.
Assist others as much as you can.**

These seem like simple suggestions, easier to understand and follow than the lofty words of "love God and love your neighbor as yourself." But in my experience, following them is not easy. I seem to constantly complain, even if only to myself, and I seldom feel I help others as much as I should. However, when I do follow this advice I find—and you may also find—that, as Jesus suggested to the man who questioned him, it is the only advice, the only two commandments I need to follow, to live a peaceful and meaningful life.

Fatherly Love

January 2024
Friends Journal

EACH YEAR, about a week before Christmas, I start to set up a small creche depicting the story of the birth of Jesus based on the story in the gospel of Luke. I have read and heard this story read many times; it has become the basis for the popular way the birth of Jesus is represented and re-enacted. The Nativity scene I own includes a small structure for the stable, a few cows and donkeys, a manger, and several figures to represent Mary, Joseph, baby Jesus, the angel, the shepherds, and the three wise men. I put them out in the order in which they appear, as if I were directing a play, and then, when the wise men (who are "borrowed" from the gospel of Matthew) depart, I put them back in the box for another year.

As I was putting the figures away last year, I had reached the point where only Joseph and baby Jesus were left when something made me stop. The little statue of Joseph depicts a middle-aged man with dark hair and a dark beard. He is kneeling, gazing down—in my mind gazing lovingly—at the baby lying before him in the manager. As I looked at the figure, I was reminded of the times I gazed lovingly at each of my two sons right after they were born. A wave of emotion passed through my body, bringing forth momentary tears of joy at the memory of those two occasions. Whether Joseph was the biological father of Jesus or not, I am convinced that he must have felt the same emotion gazing at this baby who was now his son. Suddenly I saw Joseph as a real person, as a father like me with a son he loved.

The gospels tell us little about Joseph. Some apocryphal stories say he was an older man, even in some cases a man in his eighties, who had six children from an earlier marriage—thus accounting for the reference to Jesus's brothers and sisters without abandoning the idea that Mary was a perpetual virgin. I don't see Joseph this way. I see him as a young man of typical marrying age for his time, maybe eighteen at most to Mary's fourteen or fifteen. Two teenagers experiencing the miracle of the birth of life together, an event that must have filled them both with joy and awe.

Matthew's gospel tells a different version of Jesus's birth in which Joseph plays a very significant role. It says that he is visited by angels on three occasions, more than anyone else in the gospels including Jesus. In the first, an angel tells him that Mary is pregnant by the Holy Spirit and that he should accept her and name the child Jesus. The second angel appears sometime after Jesus's birth and tells him to take his family to Egypt, and the third appears in Egypt telling him it is safe to return home.

There is no way to know which version—Luke's or Matthew's—is true, or whether they are each the invention of the gospel writer. But both suggest Joseph had reason to believe his son was something special. If so, did that affect his role as a father? Did he allow Jesus to go off to the synagogue to read Scripture, as was Jesus's preference, or require him to remain in the carpentry shop until Jesus was old enough to make his own decisions? Or, being only human like myself, perhaps he just tried to be the best father he could be, having no idea what that would lead to, and, if we are to believe the stories, not living long enough to find out.

Joseph is not the only father who appears in the gospels, but he is one of only two mentioned by name. The other is Zebedee, father of the disciples James and John. Zebedee appears for a brief instant in Matthew 4:21—the scene where Jesus is walking along the Sea of Galilee and summons James and John to follow him while they are in the boat with Zebedee mending their fishing nets. When I originally read this verse, my attention was drawn to James and John. I marveled that they could so easily walk away from their past lives. Did they know Jesus already, and he know them? Were they disciples of John the Baptist and at the river when Jesus came to be baptized? Or were they among John's followers when—as some stories say—Jesus stayed with John for a while thereafter? Or did they go simply because their friends Simon and Andrew were with him, and it looked like something more interesting to do than mending nets? Whatever the reason, their sudden departure is amazing and even more extraordinary if we assume they did not know Jesus at all, but were simply drawn by the magnetic nature of his presence and his unusual and unexpected invitation.

But when I think of this incident now, in the context of my thoughts about Joseph, it's the figure of Zebedee that draws my attention. How did he feel when both his sons jumped overboard and went off without asking permission or even saying a word of goodbye? Perhaps he shouted after them, "Come back! Where do you guys think you're going; there's work to be done!" Did he expect them to obey as good Jewish men brought up to honor father and mother should rightly have done? Or did he say, "Go with my blessing. Come back some time and tell me what you find"? Did he harbor a twinge of envy, wishing he had the freedom to abandon his own life and follow Jesus himself?

The answer to these questions, and some insight into how both Joseph and Zebedee might have seen their relationship with their sons, is suggested by a story about another father and his sons, the one in Luke 15:11–32 referred to as the story of the prodigal son.

This story has interested me for a long time because I am the father of two sons whose personalities are similar to the two sons in this story. My older son is generally the more responsible one, as is the older son in the story. This does not mean he chose to stay home and help run the farm, so to speak; he's gone off and had an adventurous life, more adventurous than my own. Nonetheless, he seems to be more grounded and responsible in his behavior. This is not to say that my younger son is irresponsible, for that would be inaccurate too. But he does seem to be more adventurous, more willing to take off on the spur of the moment to walk the Camino for a month or climb the mountain to Manchu Picchu. He is definitely the one who would not hesitate to ask me for his share of my estate to go off and pursue his own interests.

While this story is labeled "the prodigal son," it is really about the father and his relationship with his two sons. In response to his younger son's request to receive his future inheritance now so that he can go off and pursue his own interests, the father could have said, "No way; I need you here on the farm," just as Zebedee might have told his sons to come back. As a compromise, he might have given him some money for a short vacation but not his entire inheritance with no strings attached. Instead, he essentially says, "Go with my blessing. Come back some time and tell me what you find." In addition, he gives his son the resources necessary to do that.

If Jesus is telling this story to illustrate how a loving father should act, then we must also assume both Joseph and Zebedee send their sons off with a smile and a blessing. And if that is the case, it would be natural for both men to greet their sons eagerly and joyously when they return home, as the father in the parable does. In addition to giving his son a ring and a robe, I can imagine the father saying, "Tell me all about your adventures—I want to hear everything." While they are feasting on the fatted calf, the young man might enthusiastically have told his father a slightly censored version of his experiences. And when he later tells his own friends about them in more candid detail, I have no doubt they secretly wish to have the same opportunity.

In his book, *The Prophet*, Kahlil Gibran provides a wonderful description of the relationship between parents and children that is relevant to Joseph, Zebedee, and this father in the parable. It begins with the words: "Your children are not your children. They are the sons and daughters of Life's longing for itself." At the end, he uses the analogy of an archer to convey the notion of what it means to be a parent. In this analogy, the parent is the bow and the child is the arrow. The function of the bow is simply to launch the arrow. It does not determine the target, or the path the arrow will follow, or whether it will go high and long or short and low. This is the responsibility of the archer who directs both arrow and bow.

> *You are the bows from which your children as living arrows are sent forth.*
>
> *The archer sees the mark upon the path of the infinite, and He bends you with His might that His arrows may go swift and far.*
>
> *Let your bending in the archer's hand be for gladness;*
> *For even as He loves the arrow that flies, so He loves also the bow that is stable.*

Throughout the gospels, Jesus frequently refers to God as "father." Some people believe that the story of the prodigal son is intended to illustrate what he means in using this term. From that perspective the father represents God, the sons represent all of us, and the moral of the story is that God loves us no matter what we do. If, however, the story is intended to tell us that God's attitude toward us is illustrated by the father's attitude toward his son, then in addition to telling us that God will continue to love us no matter what we do, it also tells us that God wants us to enjoy our lives and to follow our dreams, our own particular destinies. The father in the parable wants his younger son to enjoy his life on his own terms. Joseph and Zebedee want the same for their sons. All three fathers allow themselves to "bend in the archer's hand [with] gladness." They send their sons off with their blessing to pursue their own destinies.

And so, we must assume that in Jesus's view the gift of life comes with God's blessing to go forth and enjoy our lives; to see what life has to offer; to explore, have adventures, pursue our own particular destinies. With that blessing come the resources to fulfill it: a beautiful earth on which to live, food and water, and friends and companions with whom to share our adventures. And I imagine God is just as eager to hear our stories when we return as were the three fathers.

It seems strange to me to have these thoughts now. My sons are in their mid-40s, both adult men with lives of their own. These ideas would have been more relevant, and more helpful, when I was younger and trying to learn how to be a loving father. So why do I find them now? Perhaps it is to encourage me to consider how I've done; was I a good bow? Did I send them off with my blessing and with resources to help them pursue their own destinies; did I greet them eagerly and with unconditional love when they returned? I can easily see the places where I might have done better, but overall, I think it would be fair to say the answer to those questions is yes. However, that's for them, not me, to judge.

But perhaps this message isn't for me at all; perhaps I am just a messenger, enlisted to pass it along to my sons to help them understand what it means to be a loving father to their children:

Be a good bow; bend in the archer's hand with gladness. Remember that once you were the arrow and what it was like to fly.

The Courage of a Caterpillar

October 2024
Friends Journal

MESSAGES IN meeting for worship almost always come to me from a source outside myself. An event, person, or something someone else says touches a place deep inside me and brings forth a thought, an insight, a message to be shared. It seems that the external influence sends off vibrations which produce a complementary vibration within me that occurs without a conscious decision on my part, much like two tuning forks vibrating in complementary harmony with one another.

That was the case today while attending meeting for worship via Zoom. One participant's profile picture was an image of a butterfly, which flashed briefly on her screen before she turned on her video to reveal herself. The butterfly was drawn in black on a white background and had blue and orange colors—whether it was a real butterfly or an artist's interpretation, I am not sure. It was a striking visual image in contrast to the squares of solemn faces on my screen, and caught my attention immediately. And just as immediately a message came forth, fully formed in my mind in a brief instant, but one that would take me several more minutes to figure out how to say, even longer to put it into words and say it, and even longer to write about it.

During the previous week I had been reading Book 39 of the Muslim scholar al-Ghazali's *Revival of the Religious Sciences*. Book 39 is about contemplation and is based on a story and hadith of Muhammad (PBUH). The story goes that Muhammad (PBUH) passed a group of followers sitting in meditation and asked them what they were doing. Meditating on God was the answer. But, he said, *you can't meditate on God. God is too vast, too unknowable. Meditate on God's creation and that will lead you to God.* Reflecting this advice, al-Ghazali's book is filled with detailed descriptions about contemplating various aspects of creation and marveling at how miraculous and mysterious creation, and therefore God, is.

After reading the book I gazed at a bouquet of flowers in a vase on my table, thinking about them in a way I hadn't done before. It takes me some effort to suck up a drink of water through a straw, but the flowers in my vase were somehow easily pulling water up through the stem and sending it out to the leaves and blossoms above. How was it doing this simple and amazing thing? I am sure a botanist knows, but I have no idea. And what happens to the water when it gets to the leaves and the blossoms and just seems to disappear? No idea about that either, but I know without the water the flowers will wither in a day.

This simple act of contemplating a common-place object I'd looked at indifferently many times before left me in awe and enabled me to see how al Ghazali could say that creation itself is the proof of the existence of God. No human intelligence or act of evolution could come up with the design and operation of even something as simple as a flower.

These thoughts were still in my mind when I looked at the image of the butterfly and considered how extraordinary it was that a butterfly existed at all—how extraordinary and miraculous is the process of a caterpillar wrapping itself in a cocoon to die, and yet not to die but to be transformed into a beautiful butterfly! While this process of transformation could be an analogy for our own death, suggesting that death is not an end but only a change of state into something new and wonderful, the message that came to me this morning was not about death but about the transformation we undergo while we live.

The caterpillar is a lowly creature. It crawls slowly across the ground or on a branch or leaf spending most of its time looking for food in order to survive. Its existence is solely material, solely about the physical world. Yet it is born with the inherent potential of becoming a butterfly. Does it know that—I mean consciously know—or is it a hidden knowledge that requires something else to stimulate it and bring it forth? I don't know. But at some point the caterpillar is called to change—and I use the word "called" in a spiritual sense, called from some source outside itself. So, it undertakes the marvelous act of creating a cocoon. Does it know that it will die in the process? Does it suffer, feel pain as it transforms? Or does it know that it won't really die but will be transformed and so undertakes the process of metamorphosis with confidence and joy? I like to think that it doesn't know the outcome; it simply knows that it *must* change and takes the risk of changing without being certain what the outcome will be. It faces its apparent death with a leap of faith.

Like the caterpillar, we are born into a material existence. We are tied to a material world, to activities necessary for our own survival. Like the caterpillar, we start out as lowly creatures. But we too are born with the inherent potential to be something else, something more. But to be that we also must take the risk of change. Many spiritual traditions refer to this type of change as a death. "You must die before you die" is a phrase often attributed to Muhammad (PBUH) and is found in a poem by Rumi. Jesus says, "You must be born again." Both phrases mean that we must overcome our attachment to and the limitations of material existence as the primary source of our being—we must overcome "the world" as George Fox puts it, the temptations that hold us back and distract us from a spiritual existence. We must die to our old self in order to become a new self, united in harmony with God. And that change may not occur without some pain and suffering, even if only the pain of severing past relationships or rejection by others who can't accept the new person we have become, as Jesus himself experienced.

What makes this process of change happen is as mysterious to me as what makes the caterpillar decide to change. It can be something that happens over time or something that happens almost instantaneously. But once it happens, a new self bursts forth as strikingly different from our old self as the butterfly is from the caterpillar. At the times that this has happened for me, I have had a feeling of light-heartedness, of being relieved of a burden I didn't know I was carrying, of joy, of a different quality of peace than I'd experienced before that encourages me to move through life with the same ease and confidence with which a butterfly floats through the air.

After I had offered these thoughts, two other participants in worship that day shared their reflections and a personal example of transformation. However, our personal transformation is not just personal. Each person who overcomes the constraints of the world, who has the courage of the caterpillar to take the risk of change—whether spiritual or personal (for in the end they are both the same)—each person who does that brings a gift as inspiring as a butterfly that encourages others to have the courage to change as well, which brings us all one step closer to the peaceful and loving world God desires.

Such Thought Have I

November 2024

In his poem, *All Souls' Night*, William Butler Yeats calls to mind several of his friends who have died. For each one, he writes a few lines describing something he remembers about them. The line I remember best is the one that describes his friend Horton's feelings after his wife's death: "One dear hope had he: / The inclemency / Of that or the next winter would be death."

From time-to-time friends who have died come to mind for no apparent reason. The ones I remember most are not those who died after a long and lingering illness or simply from old age, but the ones who died "suddenly" or "unexpectedly," as their obituaries would say. It does not matter which person comes to mind first; each is a link in a chain leading from one to another in no order until I, like Yeats, find that "Such thought, that in it bound / I need no other thing, / Wound in mind's wandering / As mummies in the mummy-cloth are wound."

Billy was the most popular boy in my high-school class. He was the star athlete on the football, basketball, and baseball teams. He was handsome and admired by boys and girls alike. He sat behind me in homeroom and frequently asked to borrow my math homework to "check" his answers. I was honored to oblige. Our town had what was called Canteen—a Saturday-night event at a gym in a park where there was ping pong, bowling, and dancing to give us teenagers something to do. Afterwards, those who had drivers' licenses and the family car went to a nearby Howard Johnsons restaurant for ice cream and conversation. One night I bumped into Billy in the parking lot. He was with two seniors (we were juniors), all three of them drinking beer while I was sipping a milkshake. We talked, then I got in my car and headed home, and they got in theirs, presumably to do the same. On a curving road with no streetlights, the driver lost control of the car. This was before seat belts. The car smashed into a large tree at a high-speed sending Billy, who was in the passenger seat, through the front windshield onto the hood of the car. The ragged edges of glass cut his body in half. He died immediately. He was 18.

I exchanged text messages with Sandy on Thursday afternoon about our upcoming pool match. He was a fine pool player and, what's more, a fine teammate. He never hesitated to step in to give a word of helpful advice when it seemed to him advice was needed. On Friday I have no doubt he said a cheerful goodbye to his colleagues at work, wishing them a pleasant weekend. Perhaps he had special plans of his own, such as a visit to his long-time girlfriend in Baltimore. On Monday, friends who were concerned that he was not taking or returning their calls went to his apartment and found him dead. I never learned the cause or actual day. He was 66.

Hal and I talked on the phone on Friday morning concerning something about his plans for the restoration of the Boyd movie theater. He was a jovial man; nothing seemed to upset his good humor or optimism, not even his frequent bankruptcies. On Saturday morning he had a heart attack and was put into a medically induced coma for a week before his family released him and he died. He was 54.

Paul L., a Quaker friend, rose early for his morning row on the Schuylkill River. He kissed his wife goodbye, then rode his bike two and a half miles to the boat house where he joined his rowing partner and rowed up the river and back. Near the end he had a massive heart attack. His rowing partner and a man in a nearby boat saved him from drowning and managed to get him to a hospital where he was put into an induced coma. But his brain had died; his family had to release him a few days later. He was 72.

Bob, also a Quaker friend, and his son Tom, offered to mow the meeting house lawn during the summer. Bob put his mower in his van and drove over; his son came by bike from his own apartment nearby. How they divided up the chores I do not know. After the work was over, they most likely shared a bottle of cold water.

It all seems uneventful, but as a father I can understand how it was a nice "bonding" experience. Bob loaded up the mower and drove on home. Before leaving, Tom called his drug dealer and arranged a pickup only a few blocks away. He rode his bike to a nearby restaurant, where he overdosed and died on the men's room floor. He was 27.

Paul C. went out one winter's day to shovel his driveway. It had been a heavy storm, leaving about two feet of snow all over Chestnut Hill. It was a damp snow and consequently quite heavy. Paul worked away until the driveway was clear. Finished, he came inside, took off his boots and coat and sat down in the living room while his wife went to make him a cup of hot tea. When she returned, he had died. He was 84.

Sally was doing various tasks around the house. Her husband, Jim, was sitting on the couch reading a magazine while their two young sons were outside in the yard playing. From time to time, she glanced out the window to make sure they were okay. She noticed that Jim had stopped reading and was laying back on the couch, apparently taking a short nap. When she called to ask him to go outside and keep an eye on the children, she got no reply. He had died. He was 75.

Kevin was clearing the breakfast dishes off the table. Luke usually spent the weekends at Kevin's apartment, and the weekdays at his own. He was sitting on the couch leafing through a magazine. As Kevin walked back and forth, he noticed Luke had leaned back and seemed to be taking a nap. After he had loaded the dishwasher and finished cleaning up, he returned to the living room and discovered that Luke was not taking a nap; he had died. He was 59.

Mike and I played on a tennis team together for several years. We met at practice and at matches, and occasionally saw one another at gay clubs. Despite this infrequent contact, I considered him a good friend. He lost his job, couldn't find another, and his life began to unravel. His longtime boyfriend left him. I could tell he was in trouble one day when he showed up at practice having been absent for many weeks. But I had a meeting to get to that day and couldn't stay to talk with him. Several weeks later his former boyfriend called to say he had gone over to Mike's house to check on him and found that he had died in bed, probably several days before. The cause was pneumonia; he had lost his health insurance and apparently didn't know what to do. He was 45.

Mike's death haunted me for months. I felt it was my fault; I knew he needed help, but did not offer it. One night following his death, my boyfriend and I were at a dance club, dancing in the middle of a crowded floor. I saw Mike enter and walk along the side heading to a bar in an area behind the dance floor. Those are the right words: I saw him. He was dressed as he always was—tight black t-shirt and jeans. Shortly later he came back on the other side of the room and waved to me as he was leaving. This was something he did whenever we found ourselves out in the same place together. He then turned, walked through the wall, and disappeared. I felt he had returned to tell me everything was okay, and I should stop worrying. I did, but I haven't forgotten him or forgiven myself for my failure.

Doug and I were lovers for about a year. He quickly met Bob after we split up, and they had a wonderful relationship for about five years. They discovered they each had AIDS at the same time. Bob died first. Doug was a Presbyterian minister, divorced with three children and a not-very-supportive ex-wife. He couldn't tell anyone he was gay—let alone that he had AIDS—for fear of losing his job, his health insurance, and the partial custody of his children. He told everyone he had a rare liver disease, and I guess they believed him. When he had to go to the hospital as a result of some complication, I tried to visit him each day on my way home from work. On this particular day I found his arms strapped to the side of the bed. The nurses said he kept pulling out the oxygen tubes and other tubes to which he was connected. His mind was finally gone to dementia; we couldn't even converse. I had to leave to go home and relieve the babysitter who looked after my sons when they came home from school. We were in the middle of dinner when the phone rang. Another friend who also helped look after Doug called to say Doug had died about an hour after I had left. He was 45.

Several years later I went to see a display of the AIDS quilt. While walking around I saw a blue panel with the names "Bob and Doug" in small letters. It could have been any couple, but I was sure it was for them. I also noticed that Dignity Philadelphia, an organization of gay Catholics whose services Doug and I often attended, had made panels for some of its members. Rounding the corner, I saw one with a red background and white letters and his full name. It was such I shock I fell to my knees and burst into tears. It was as if he had finally, and proudly, claimed his true identify.

Ted had been having health problems for several years. His balance was poor and when we had lunch together, he would ask to hold my arm as we walked the few blocks from his house to the restaurant. Otherwise, he was mentally sharp and full of his usual good humor. I knew he was also having some memory problems, but they didn't seem very severe to me. After he died his wife held a "memorial reception," I guess I'd call it. She greeted me at the door and immediately said, "He took his own life." It was like having a glass of ice water thrown in my face. He was 85.

Dick had early-stage dementia. Once on a plane trip to New York from New Mexico, he got off the plane in Atlanta and wandered lost in the airport for several hours before he was found. One evening at his home in Santa Fe, he told his wife he was going out for a short walk. It was just before sundown, a beautiful time of day in that area. I can imagine that after walking a distance from the house he might have stopped to admire what must have been a colorful sunset before he shot and killed himself. He was 78.

My sister Peg, short for Margaret, was told by her doctor that they had exhausted all possible treatments for her cancer. "Get your life in order," he said, giving her about six months to live. She wanted a family reunion, so a few weeks later I arranged for her, her husband, and their two sons to go to Boston where our mother and our brother, his wife and two daughters lived. Then I and my two sons drove up to be with them for a few days. I don't remember what we did, but we all enjoyed being together despite the circumstances. Leaving was very hard for me, but that's another story. After we left, Peg and her family went to my brother's house for dinner. When done, she sat in a reclining chair in the living room and appeared to nap while the children played outside. But she had slipped into a coma. My brother rented a hospital bed, and she rested peacefully in his living room for three or four days before she died. She was 49.

My sister's death was heartbreaking for my mother. In the weeks that followed, she frequently said she was ready for God to take her. One afternoon she took her older sister shopping. I am sure that was just an excuse to give her sister, who was suffering from early-stage dementia, something to do. My mother was always helping others. She came home to the senior-citizen apartment where she lived alone after my father died, had dinner with some friends, went to bed, and died in her sleep. At the wake one of her fellow residents said to me, "That's the way I want to go." She was 84.

I could go on. Gray went into the hospital for minor surgery and died of complications a day or two later at age 69. Paul and I visited Bill on Thursday. He was mentally sharp although still recovering from several falls. It was a nice visit. He died the following day at age 94. And then there are my more famous acquaintances: Lou Kahn, returning from a trip to India, went from JFK airport to Penn Station to get a train to Philadelphia. Not feeling well, he went into the men's room, collapsed, and died on the floor at age 73. Frank Rizzo had just won the Republican nomination for mayor of Philadelphia, hoping to secure an unprecedented third term. He wasn't feeling well so left his staff meeting, went into the restroom, collapsed, and died on the floor at age 70. John B. Kelly Jr., an Olympic rower, went out for his morning run. He was found dead on the sidewalk three blocks from his home. He was 57.

There is something to be said for a sudden death. No weeks or months of pain, no in and out of the hospital. But perhaps I remember all these sudden deaths so frequently because, unlike my mother's friend, that's the kind of death I fear. I want to be able to say one last goodbye to my sons and partner; I want one last hug, one last smile, one last opportunity to say I love you even if that requires enduring some pain. But the form of death is not something we control any more than we control the time or place. All that, I believe, has been determined before we are born and will come at the right moment, the moment when it's time for our soul to move on to prepare for the next incarnation. I hope that time for me is still many years away. But I am aware that I live in a state of precarious uncertainty, and yet I still must live—not with the desperation that tomorrow may be my last day but with the determination to use each day well, so that when that last one finally comes, I can say I enjoyed the gift of life to the fullest.

Acknowledgments

I am grateful for the support and assistance of two groups of people: those who supported me during the writing of these reflections and essays and those who assisted me with this publication.

SOURCES OF SUPPORT AND INSPIRATION

Marcelle Martin and Jorge Arauz encouraged me to write reports of my experiences while we participated in the prayer vigil for peace. Robert Dockhorn, senior editor of *Friends Journal* at the time, published several in the *Journal*, which encouraged me to submit a selection to Pendle Hill, ten of which were published in 2001 as Pamphlet 358 and are included here with permission of Pendle Hill Publications.

Reflections written during the Covid-19 pandemic were supported by readers from several Quaker meetings in Philadelphia; Mickey Edgerton was my most faithful reader and a constant source of encouragement. Jon Landau suggested I submit them to Pendle Hill, where Janaki Spickard Keeler helped me select and edit nine, which were published in 2022 as Pamphlet

469 and are included here with permission of Pendle Hill Publications.

Martin Kelley, senior editor of *Friends Journal*, has been a constant source of support for my writing, for which I am most grateful. Sixteen of the essays in this collection were published in *Friends Journal*.

ASSISTANCE WITH THIS PUBLICATION

Laura Simmons of Simmons Creative Communications re-edited all the essays and provided much helpful guidance; Fred Courtright of The Permissions Co. reviewed my use of quotations from other sources. Mark Willie designed the fine cover, with a photograph by Andrew Gallery; Douglas Gordon designed the interior, prepared the text for publication, converted it to an eBook, and managed the process of placing it online. Doug's services were indispensable in enabling me to publish the book in the form I wanted. Paul Dry of Paul Dry Books introduced me to Doug and Fred and provided helpful advice at a critical moment. Thank you all.

John Andrew Gallery
Philadelphia, January 2025

Citations

Note about dates: The month and year given for reflections published in Pendle Hill pamphlets, and for unpublished reflections, is the month and year in which the reflection was written. For those published in *Friends Journal*, it is the month and year of publication, which was usually a few months later than the month in which the reflection was written.

19. Frank Herbert, *Dune* (Penguin Books, 2016), 10.
23. Fred Small, "Cranes Over Hiroshima," track 5 on *No Limit*, Rounder Records, 1985; Pine Barrens Music, BMI, 1983.
26. H.H. The Dalai Lama, Forward to Thich Nhat Hanh, *Peace is Every Step* (Bantam Books, 1992), 19–20.
36. Interview with Ed Bradley; see also, Lou Michel and Dan Herbeck, *American Terrorist: Timothy McVeigh and the Oklahoma City Bombing* (Regan Books, 2001), 351, 380.
43-44. Loren Eiseley, *The Immense Journey* (Vintage, 1959), 19–20.
49. Thomas Merton, *The Hidden Ground of Love: Letters on Religious Experience and Social Concerns*, ed. William H. Shannon (Farrar, Straus, Giroux, 1985), 294–97.

53. Fr. Ken Untemer, for a homily by Cardinal John Dearden, 1979 (romerotrust.org.uk).
58. Lloyd Stone/Georgia Harkness, *A Song of Peace: A Patriotic Song* (Lorenz Publishing Company, 1934).
64. George Fox, *The Journal of George Fox*, ed. John L. Nickalls (Britain Yearly Meeting; printed by Philadelphia Yearly Meeting and Quaker Books, 2005), 263.
65. Thomas Merton, *The Hidden Ground of Love*, 33.
71-77. Ernesto Che Guevara, *The Motorcycle Diaries* (Ocean Press, 2003), 31; Walter Salles, The Motorcycle Diaries, Focus Features, 2004.
74. George Fox, *Journal*, 2.
78-79. Norman Jewison, et al, Moonstruck, MGM, 1988.
83. *Hua Hu Ching, The Unknown Teachings of Lao Tzu*, trans. Brian Walker (HarperSanFrancisco, 1992), 4.
84. Neale Donald Walsch, *The New Revelations: A Conversation with God* (Atria Books, 2002), 321.
86. al-Ghazali, *On the Duties of Brotherhood*, trans. Muhtar Holland (Overlook Press, 1976), 58.
87. M. Scott Peck, *The Road Less Traveled* (Random House, 1991), 81.
89. William Penn, *Some Fruits of Solitude*, 1693, #545 (Applewood Books), 94.
89. *Hua Hu Ching*, 6.
94. Jean-Yves Leloup, *The Gospel of Philip*, trans. Joseph Rowe (Inner Traditions, 2004), 15, 57.
95-103. Phil Alden Robinson, Field of Dreams, Universal City Studios, 1989; based on the novel *Shoeless Joe* by W.P. Kinsella (Houghton Mifflin, 1982).

Citations

- 96-97, 99. Paul A. Lacey, *Leading and Being Led*, Pendle Hill Pamphlet 264 (Pendle Hill Publications, 1985), 18, 31–32.
- 105. Albert Camus, *The Myth of Sisyphus*, trans. Justin O'Brien (Vintage Books, 1955), 89, 91.
- 109. "Companions on the Journey," an Interview with Harold Kushner, in *Sacred Journey: The Journal of Fellowship in Prayer* (vol 50:1, April/May 2008), 12, 13.
- 110. Tirmidhī, Muḥammad ibn 'Īsá (Vol 4:11), Hadith 2517.
- 112. Henry David Thoreau, *The Heart of Thoreau's Journals*, ed. Odell Shepard (Dover, 1961), 2.
- 112. Dhammapada, *The Sayings of the Buddha*, trans. Thomas Byron (Shambhala Pocket Classics, 1993), 25.
- 129. Bob Thiele and George David Weiss, "What a Wonderful World," (Larry Spier Music LLC o/b/o Abilene Music LLC, Range Rover Music Inc., Quartet Music, 1967)
- 136. Walsch, *The New Revelations*, 131.
- 136. *The Way of Life (According to Lao-tzu)*, trans. Witter Bynner (Capricorn Books, 1962), 67.
- 136. T.E. Lawrence, *Seven Pillars of Wisdom* (Doubleday, Doran & Company, 1935), 39.
- 140. Leonard Cohen, *Poems and Songs*, ed. Robert Faggen, Everyman Library Pocket Poets (Alfred A. Knopf, 2011), 188.
- 141. Richard Carlson, *Don't Sweat the Small Stuff... and It's All Small Stuff* (Hachette, 1997), 85.
- 143. Justin E. Stone, *Tai Chi Chih! Joy Thru Movement* (Good Karma Publishing, 1996).

- 150. Lin Chi, in *The Zen Teachings of Master Lin-Chi*, trans. Berton Watson (Columbia University Press, 1999), 52.
- 149–50. Herman Hesse, *Siddhartha*, trans. Susan Bernofsky (Modern Library, 2008), 123.
- 160. Marcus Aurelius, *Meditations*, trans. Gregory Hayes (Modern Library, 2002), 34, 62.
- 160. "Chief Seattle" statement by Ted Perry, *Home*, Southern Baptist Radio and Television Commission, 1972.
- 160. *The Meditations of Marcus Aurelius Antoninus*, trans. A.S. Farquharson (Oxford University Press, 1992), 37, 57, 117.
- 161. Marcus Aurelius, *Meditations*, trans. Maxwell Staniforth (Penguin Books, 1964), 59, 66.
- 163–64. *The Qur'an*, trans. Tarif Khalidi (Viking, 2008), 364.
- 165–66. Daniel Day-Lewis in Terrence Rafferty, "The Film That Runs in The Family. Both Families, in Fact," *New York Times*, March 27, 2005.
- 172. Jason Mraz, "Look for the Good," track 1 on *Look for the Good*, Interrabang, 2020.
- 173. Jimmy McHugh and Dorothy Fields, "On the Sunny Side of the Street," Sony/ATV Music Publishing LLC, 1930.
- 173. Thich Nhat Hanh, *Peace is Every Step* (Bantam Books, 1991), 41.
- 182. William Shakespeare, *Hamlet*, Act II, Scene ii.
- 185. Ralph H. Blum, *The Book of Runes* (St. Martin's Press, 1993), 143.
- 192. George Fox, *Journal*, 11.

201. Robert Leach, *The Inward Journey of Isaac Penington* (Pendle Hill Pamphlet 29, 1945), 28.
206. David Bentley Hart, *The New Testament* (Yale University Press, 2017), 10.
210. Alexander Lowen, M.D., *Joy: The Surrender to the Body and to Life* (Arkana/The Penguin Group, 1995), 301.
216. Duane Michals, "The Spirit Leaves the Body," 1968, published in *Real Dreams* (Addison House, 1969).
222. Rumi, *Rumi: Selected Poems*, trans. Coleman Barks (Penguin Books, 2005), 109.
227. Michael Hirst, writer, *The Tudors* (Season 4, Episode 4, "Natural Ally," aired May 2, 2010) Phase 4 Films and Take 5 Productions in association with Showtime Television, television series.
230. Attributed to many individuals including Nelson Mandela, Anne Lamott, Alice May, and Alcoholics Anonymous.
232. Alexander Pope, *An Essay on Criticism*, 1711.
242. Kahlil Gibran, *The Prophet* (Knopf, 1923), 17–18.
246. al-Ghazali, *The Book of Contemplation, Book 39 of The Revival of the Religious Sciences*, trans. Muhammad Isa Waley (Fons Vitae, 2021).
250. William Butler Yeats, *The Selected Poems of W. B. Yeats* (The Macmillan Company, 1964), 224–226.

ABOUT THE AUTHOR

John Andrew Gallery lives in Philadelphia, where he attends the Chestnut Hill Friends Meeting. After retiring from a distinguished career in city planning, community development, and historic preservation, John turned his interests to the ministry of writing. He is the author of many *Friends Journal* articles, four Pendle Hill pamphlets, two self-published pamphlets, and the self-published book *Living in the Kingdom of God*. For more information about John and his spiritual writing, visit www.johnandrewgallery.com.

www.ingramcontent.com/pod-product-compliance
Lightning Source LLC
LaVergne TN
LVHW041624060526
838200LV00040B/1422